PRAISE FOR *A DOSE OF POSITIVITY*

"Mike Diamond is more than a writer and teacher—he is a wellness revolutionary and a force for change. *A Dose of Positivity* is a must-read to fast track your life."

—Kelly Cutrone, founder and CEO of People's Revolution and *New York Times* bestselling author

"*A Dose of Positivity* is a book that will help anyone who feels stuck and needs inspiration and motivation. Mike Diamond's courage and resilience offers a path forward for all of us. He truly walks the talk and shows us simple, powerful ways to heal and thrive. *A Dose of Positivity* has the power to transform our individual and collective lives."

—Shauna Shapiro, PhD, author of *Good Morning, I Love You: Mindfulness and Self-Compassion to Rewire the Mind*

"*A Dose of Positivity* by Mike Diamond easily describes and outlines how to approach life in a way that creates incredible changes. I found it inspiring, entertaining, and effective."

—Danny Nucci, actor, writer, director, and producer

"Mike Diamond is the real deal. *A Dose of Positivity* will give you all the tools you need to live an extraordinary life."

—David Yazbez, Grammy- and Tony Award-winning writer and producer

"If *A Dose of Positivity* doesn't inspire and motivate you, nothing will. This book is packed with great stories, tools, and strategies for everyone. Get your dose now!"

—Chris Booker, radio and TV personality

"Legit. Since birth, for the rest of our lives, we all chase a DOSE. Wrong thinking forces us to experiment with unhealthy things to obtain it. This book will 'legit' change your thinking so you can finally get the DOSE you've always wanted but was out of reach. I want to 'be like Mike.' Well done!"

—Rob Hannley, publisher, *Recovery Today* magazine

"Mike Diamond is a combination of an Outlier and Sage. The practical methods he teachers, and what he outlays in *A Dose of Positivity*, can help anyone transform their life. Mike travels on an ancient path of wisdom, sharing his life, pain, struggles, and victories through incredible transformative stories and lessons. This is the book of 2023, trust me on that!"

—Adam Jablin, bestselling author, entrepreneur, and addiction specialist

"*A Dose of Positivity*, by Mike Diamond, is a cocktail of content that educates and empowers, not with unrealistic bars to meet but with real life lessons learned. Get Yourself A Dose Now!"

—Allie Merrick McGuire, chief editor and one of the founders of *AwareNow* magazine

"So many desperately want change, but they don't know what to do. I love how Mike not only shares his personal story and real-life experience but also provides tangible actions people can take to actually create lasting change."

—Wesley Geer, founder and CEO, Rock to Recovery

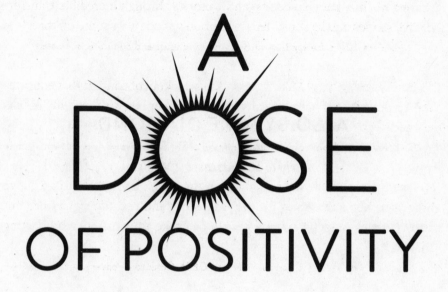

A DOSE OF POSITIVITY

ALSO BY MIKE DIAMOND

7 Steps to an Unbreakable Mindset

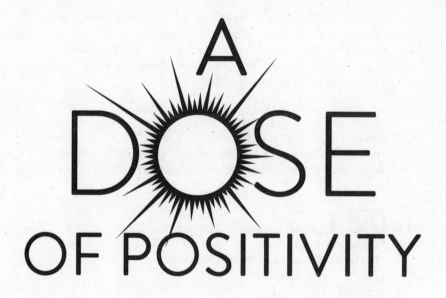

A DOSE OF POSITIVITY

Tools, Techniques, and Strategies
to Live Life on Your Terms

MIKE DIAMOND

Matt Holt Books
An Imprint of BenBella Books, Inc.
Dallas, TX

A Dose of Positivity copyright © 2023 by Michael Diamond

Matt Holt is an imprint of BenBella Books, Inc.
10440 N. Central Expressway
Suite 800
Dallas, TX 75231
benbellabooks.com
Send feedback to feedback@benbellabooks.com

BenBella and *Matt Holt* are federally registered trademarks.

Printed in the United States of America
10 9 8 7 6 5 4 3 2 1

Library of Congress Control Number: 2022040503
ISBN 9781637743133 (hardcover)
ISBN 9781637743140 (electronic)

Editing by Gregory Newton Brown
Copyediting by Lydia Choi
Proofreading by Madeline Grigg and Ariel Fagiola
Text design and composition by Aaron Edmiston
Cover design by Brigid Pearson
Printed by Lake Book Manufacturing

For my amazing wife, Kim, and incredible son, Orlando.

CONTENTS

Foreword by David Meltzer xi
Introduction: Running into the Flames 1

PART ONE

CHAPTER 1 The Value of Change 7
CHAPTER 2 Choosing Empowerment 21

PART TWO

CHAPTER 3 Reframe Your Perspective 41
CHAPTER 4 The Importance of a Positive Outlook 59
CHAPTER 5 Your Purpose in Life 75
CHAPTER 6 Perseverance and Patience 91
CHAPTER 7 Influential People 107
CHAPTER 8 Bring Place to You by Mastering Time 125
CHAPTER 9 Finalize Your Plan for Success with
Self-Discipline and Spirituality 145
CHAPTER 10 Parting Words: Call a Time-Out 167

Epilogue 175
Acknowledgments 179
Endnotes 183

FOREWORD BY DAVID MELTZER

We cannot control everything in our lives to ensure that they consist of only positivity, but there are three areas we *can* control to give us the "dose of positivity" we need. The first is our mindset, the mental framework with which we approach our lives. Next is our heartset, simply described as how we feel. Finally, there is our handset, the actions that we take. The pragmatic guidance from my good friend Mike Diamond found in this book will not only help you maximize each of these areas of your life but also empower you to surround yourself with the right people, the right ideas, and the right habits.

I was lucky enough to meet Mike in early 2020, when he came to my office in Irvine, California, to record an episode as a guest on my podcast, *The Playbook*. In fact, this would be one of the last in-person podcasts I would record for a long stretch, due to the onset of COVID-19. But the timing was not the most memorable part of our first interaction—it was how my experience with Mike made me feel. He and I were so aligned in our ideas and our frequency that it was as if we had known each other for decades (or lifetimes). We both immediately knew that our relationship would extend past a single podcast episode, and we agreed to get together soon to work on ideas. What neither of us could have planned for, however, was the onset of a pandemic. So we decided to create a virtual show that we would host together, bringing as much value as we could to our respective audiences. What evolved out of this idea was the live-streamed show *Office Hours,* and my episodes featuring Mike as cohost became known as the *DOSE from David & Diamond.* With a litany of entrepreneurs, thought leaders, and executives from all walks of life sharing their best strategies and advice for success and fulfillment, this platform continued to grow, with *Office Hours* eventually becoming a late-night entrepreneurial television series on Bloomberg and Apple TV that has already aired two seasons.

My relationship with Mike served as a catalyst for this success, just like this book can serve as a catalyst for changing your life. He will give you the tools to improve your mindset, heartset, and handset, but it will be up to you to use them. To start, he will help you delve into your current mindset, reflecting and taking a personal inventory. This inventory is crucial because it empowers you to focus on what you want and value most in life, rather than what you do not want (or what others might want for you). From there, you can decide on a trajectory for yourself and set your mid-term and long-term goals.

We can also develop rapid improvement in our heartset, or emotions, especially by understanding what it means to get a "DOSE" of feel-good chemicals. Learning about the activities and emotions that release dopamine, oxytocin, serotonin, and endorphins in our bodies enables us to better control these processes. You can even reprogram your mind with the strategies found within this book when you apply them consistently and persistently. When you understand how these chemicals work, you can combine them with the final component: your handset (otherwise known as your actions).

Our habits, much like the people and ideas we surround ourselves with, have a major impact on our perspective or reality. Even more importantly, our positive and negative habits aggregate over time. We may expect positive results from our positive habits almost immediately, but the truth is that it takes time and consistency for them to work. Conversely, we rarely consider the negative consequences of our negative habits, like smoking or drinking, but over time, the impacts from these habits become exponentially stronger in our lives. This makes having positive habits, those which provide us with a DOSE of positivity in the right way at the right time, absolutely crucial. These habitual actions are what let us stay aligned to our core values and live with abundance, clarity, intention, and gratitude. They realign us when we lose sight of what's important and empower us to connect with our sources of inspiration.

I believe that happiness comes from the enjoyment of the consistent (that is, you do it every day) and persistent (that is, you don't quit) pursuit of your potential. The tools provided by Mike in *A Dose of Positivity* will undoubtedly make a impact on your life, just as he has made an impact on mine. And if you are looking to add more positivity to your life: be kind to your future self and do good deeds.

David Meltzer is the cofounder of Sports 1 Marketing and the former CEO of the renowned Leigh Steinberg Sports & Entertainment agency, which inspired the movie *Jerry Maguire*. David is also a three-time international best-selling author, a Marshall Goldsmith Top 100 business coach, and the host of the top entrepreneur podcast *The Playbook*.

David serves as the executive producer of the Bloomberg and Apple TV television series *2 Minute Drill* and *Office Hours*, as well as of *Entrepreneur*'s number-one digital business show, *Elevator Pitch*. He is featured in many books, movies, and TV shows, such as *World's Greatest Motivators*, *Think and Grow Rich: The Legacy*, and *Beyond the Secret*, airing on Amazon Prime. David has been recognized by *Variety* magazine as its Sports Humanitarian of the Year and was awarded an Ellis Island Medal of Honor.

Introduction

RUNNING INTO THE FLAMES

H ow did you come to write this book?" my publisher asked me.

I took a deep breath and replied (paraphrasing here):

Born in Perth, Australia, I got off to a rough start, battling undiagnosed dyslexia and using drugs and alcohol starting at age twelve. But Lady Luck was on my side in 1997 when I won a Green Card lottery ticket and moved to Miami.

Shortly after arriving, I landed a role on the CBS sitcom *Grapevine*. After that, I moved to New York City and guest-starred on *Sex and the City*. Next, I wrote, created, and starred in a VH1 show with former Stone Temple Pilots front man Scott Weiland. Meanwhile, between NYC and Los Angeles, I performed stand-up comedy at Carolines on Broadway and the Comedy Store. An introduction to the tattoo world led to a role on *Miami Ink*, and I starred on Season 3 of *NY Ink*. Back in my hometown, I wrote, directed, produced, and starred in *Bondi Ink Tattoo Crew*.

Although I've had plenty of highs along the way, I've also battled cocaine and alcohol addiction for the majority of my life . . . until April 16,

2006, the day I got sober for good. And in 2017, my appendix burst, sending my body into toxic shock. The doctors gave me a fifty-fifty chance of surviving the surgery, which would include removing my colon and attaching a colostomy bag that I'd have to wear for the rest of my life. More on that story later.

Currently, I perform nationwide onstage as a motivational speaker and coach, doing keynote talks and kick-off meetings for companies such as Aflac and AXA Equitable in front of audiences of over a thousand people. I am the cocreator of a program called Impacted Youth, and I tour LA County schools to motivate, educate, and inspire our youth to make empowering choices. In 2019, I was on stage more than 250 times, and I was booked solid for 2020 before the pandemic hit.

But that didn't slow me down. I took my message to the internet, connecting with people on Zoom and doing seminars, interventions, and live coaching sessions up to five times a day. I also cocreated a weekly podcast with *Recovery Today* magazine, where incredible guests come on to talk about their experiences in recovery. Every Wednesday I do a podcast series called *DOSE from David & Diamond* with entrepreneur and master coach David Meltzer. And on Fridays, I host a weekly series called Friday Fire to help lift people's spirits before they head into the weekend.

But it's not about me. I told my publisher I didn't write this book for me; it's for and about *you*. While my story is part of the journey, I wrote this book to show others how to live life on their terms, each and every day. I am going to give you the tools that worked extremely well for me, tools that will help you tap into your higher power, learn to choose empowerment every time, and *be* the change you want instead of waiting for the change to happen to you.

In part one of the book, I'll tell you my story. To give you a quick overview of my path: I was born in the most isolated capital city in the world, grew up in an abusive household, and came to America with nothing. I was an undiagnosed dyslexic and halfway to being an addict. I took a shot and created TV shows. I opened nightclubs and restaurants in the biggest cities in the world. I did it by doing the work, regardless of how I was feeling, and never quitting. Along the way, I watched drugs and alcohol claim the lives of some of my best friends and felt that fate coming for me as well.

I got myself sober despite being in the nightclub business. While it wasn't an environment that supported being a nondrinker, I stuck it out until I'd saved enough money to move on and start building a new life and career. And I never relapsed. No one did an intervention on me. I didn't detox in a fancy rehab facility. I made the choice to get sober and turn my life around. I became greater than my environment and was successful because I had faith in my resiliency and had the tools to change my habits.

I don't fear the future, have no regrets from the past, and continue to take responsibility and make amends whenever I get off track and unintentionally harm others. I've learned to live in the moment, learn from my mistakes, and strive to never repeat what doesn't move me forward. I look at what I want and why I want it—then I work out how to get it. Right now, I want the same for *you*.

In part two, I'll shift the focus to your story. I'll share the tools to help you close the gap between where you are now and where you want to be. Through my personal experiences and my years as a motivational speaker, sobriety and recovery coach, and mentor to teens and adults struggling with addiction and trauma, I've found there are nine main ingredients that can help us get unstuck, start self-actualizing, learn to live large, and reach our full potential in all areas of life. I'll take you through each, chapter by chapter, using a combination of personal experience, historical examples, and easy-to-act-on techniques and tactics.

We need to reset as the world resets. Years of a pandemic, race riots, looting, and a country on its knees . . . this is not the America I used to know. Ask yourself this question now: "Am I ready to change?" If you're still reading this, you are obviously open and committed to shifting your life.

What would it mean for you to achieve your goals and dreams and become the best person that you could possibly be? I truly believe we are all here for a reason. But what is that reason? I say we all have a *role* and a *purpose* in life. Right now, more than ever, is the time to find them.

I'm going to provide you with a lot of viable information and workable strategies. I will tell you about the things I have experienced that work. I don't have a PhD from Stanford, MIT, or Yale. I was lucky to graduate high school. I don't need to test on other people or lab rats. I test on myself to see what works and what doesn't. And if you are willing to put in the effort, you won't just succeed—you'll excel.

There is an energy inside us all that controls the universe. I call it our Source, and throughout my life it has helped teach me more than any academic degree ever could. You can think of it as our guiding intuition or infinite intelligence . . . that thing inside us that knows more than we do if we can just learn to hear it. If we slow down, listen up, and get a natural DOSE of that energy, we have the chance to truly change. My goal is to show you what's possible, to show you how to become greater than the present you by letting go of the past and shifting your perception to create the future you want. Later in the book, we'll fully unpack what it means to call in a DOSE of positivity, but essentially, it all starts with you: identifying who and where you want to be, who and where you are now, and what you need to do to bridge those two people.

I know there are thousands of books that have been written on purpose, goals, values, rules, laws of attraction—the list goes on. I consider myself a science project. I learn what works by testing it. Thus, I'm going to save you a lot of time and money by presenting only the info and techniques that have been proven (by me) to work. Everything I'm advocating for you, I've done myself—with highly satisfactory results. And if I can do things that seem extraordinary, so can you; at the end of the day, I'm just an ordinary guy from Perth who's worked hard to reach his dreams and overcome his obstacles.

Some people believe change only happens through pain and suffering. I believe change happens when we commit to doing the work. Some people want a trophy for running out of the burning building. But who is willing to run *into* the flames? This book is about doing the work deep in the fires of change, where real success resides. My publisher seemed convinced by my passion, and I hope you will be, too.

Reaching our full potential isn't about resources; it's about being resourceful. I'm living proof of what can be done with a flexible mindset and the desire to pay attention, practice the following techniques, and become the best version of oneself.

Are you ready?

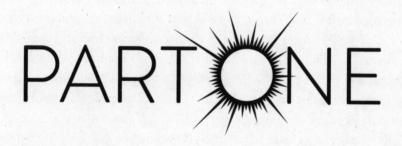

Chapter 1

THE VALUE OF CHANGE

Whether we like it or not, you and I have manifested our reality up to this point. As I sit here at my writing desk, in this present moment, I can either accept that reality—or not. It's a simple choice, but a massive one—to either believe that I have control over my mind and the choices I make, or that the world controls me.

Perhaps the hardest pill in life to swallow is the pill of taking responsibility for our present reality. We have manifested everything around us by how we choose to think, feel, and act. Our reality in this present moment has been built by the decisions we have made and the actions we have taken.

It's so easy to blame our past, parents, teachers, neighbors, the government, lack of money, lack of resources, or lack of education. We could go on forever and ever placing blame elsewhere. Trust me—I did it for years, and it got me nowhere.

So what happens when you stop blaming other people and situations and start taking responsibility for this life that you're continually creating?

As I write this, more than ever, things have become very real for me. I'm sitting in my house in Los Angeles. It's April 16, 2020, and I have been sober for exactly fourteen years. I'd like to go out and celebrate that achievement with friends and family, but we are in the middle of a pandemic. COVID-19 is spreading like a wildfire throughout the world. Life as we know it has changed, and it will be different forever. Cities are shut down. People are getting sick and dying. Businesses are gone. Jobs are gone. And people are coming undone. Like so many addicts who are now telling themselves they need the comfort of their drug of choice to get through this, the old me would be madly self-medicating with cocaine and alcohol just to get by.

But now I don't need to do that. For the first time in my life, I can say I am not worried about the future because I have the tools to easily adapt to it. It took me fourteen long years to acquire them, but I'm going to condense and simplify them for you in this book. And I guarantee you're going to have fun along the way. I have done the work to go from the hopeless addict I was to the self-made man I am today. I have a wonderful family. I am an accomplished athlete. And I have a successful business empire built on both my experiences and failures. I've made meaning in my life by bringing all kinds of people out of their despair and disillusionment into meaningful and fulfilling lives. I want the same for you.

Before I show you how I've reached a place of balance and full belief in myself, you need to know where I was. It isn't a pretty picture, and it might even shock people who have only known me as I am now.

NYC, SEPTEMBER 11, 2001: 9:15 AM

I'd finished a long late-night shift as the front-door host at the famous nightclub Bungalow 8 and was sound asleep. I was abruptly woken by my then-wife, Vanessa, who told me that terrorists had crashed two passenger airlines into the Twin Towers of the World Trade Center.

I shot her a blank stare, thinking she was playing some kind of a joke on me. My schedule was nocturnal, and I usually got home around 5 AM and slept till noon. I didn't take her seriously, and I think my response was,

"Yeah, look, okay—they tried this nonsense once before with the trucks in the parking lot," and then a laugh. I badly needed more sleep. But she kept bugging me.

Finally, I went into the living room and looked at the TV. The replayed image of planes hitting the towers looked surreal. I tossed my hands in the air. "Come on . . . you gotta be kidding me. This is a movie, right?"

Her response was simple. "Then why is it on every channel?"

I began clicking the remote, still a little dazed. *Son of a bitch! She's right.* The same nightmare vision was on every station.

At the time, I lived on Thirteenth Street and First Avenue in Manhattan's East Village. It's a place where you get used to the sound of fire trucks passing by. But the inordinate number of trucks speeding down the streets that day with their sirens blaring was on another level altogether. Still, it didn't fully register for me.

We had access to the rooftop in our apartment building, and I knew I could see the Twin Towers from there. I said to my wife, who was now pacing like a woman possessed, "Please calm down. I'll go up and take a look."

On my way to the roof, my building seemed eerily calm. I didn't really think anything of it until I reached the rooftop. It was packed with people.

And then it happened: one of the towers started to come down. I can still vividly remember watching it fall. People on the rooftop were freaking out. Some were screaming. I just stood there in utter shock. It still looked like a movie—a postapocalyptic one.

For as far as I could see in all directions, it was sheer bedlam. All these years later, and I still can't explain the madness. It was just pure insanity. Sirens, people running everywhere but going nowhere . . . just mass hysteria.

I went downstairs, looked at Vanessa with a stunned expression, and said, "Well, you were right. Shit just got real."

Anyone who lived in NYC at the time will tell you how insanely bizarre it was. Planes seemed to be going down all over the country, one after another, not just in the city.

Me? I came undone.

Up to that point, I'd been on and off with my drinking. I'd had a strange relationship with alcohol. Even though we'd been close friends since I was twelve years old, I'd never really thought I had a problem with it. After all, I could power through a bender like it was no biggie. God, was I wrong. Lesson one: not taking personal inventory in life and looking honestly at our assets and liabilities can be a dangerous choice. I'd soon learn this the hard way.

My other good buddy was cocaine. Well, what can I say about coke? It's nicknamed the "devil's dandruff" for good reason. Look, anyone who says you can't get addicted doing a drug for the first time is full of it—and has clearly never snorted or smoked cocaine. I did my first line of coke and never looked back. If you've never tried it, *don't*. Trust me, just don't. You'll love it and hate yourself for it at the same time.

Back then, New York City was a nonstop party, and I was around a lot of incredible people. To give you a brief history, Jason Strauss, one of the owners of the Tao group, was a promoter at the Chaos nightclub back then. Scott Harrison, who would later get out of the business and start charity: water, was also a promoter, along with actor Danny A. Abeckaser. The list goes on. Suffice to say, at that time I knew all the right people.

I was working on music projects and going to acting auditions. I had a showcase booked at a venue called Joe's Pub. I'd been playing shows in various NYC clubs and doing quite well writing songs and trying to get a record deal. I also worked at two of the hottest nightclubs in NYC, Chaos and Bungalow 8.

I was the door guy. Yep, I had the job of being the dick who told you, "Not tonight, buddy."

There was an A-team of door dicks back then in NYC. Wass Stevens, Allison Melnick, and a handful of others. It didn't take me long to figure out that "door guy" (even at the A-team level) was not going to get me anywhere fast. Still, there were a lot of perks. I was making good money and dreaming of conquering the world. I was just an upstart from a small town on the other side of the world trying to make it big in the city that never sleeps.

However, after 9/11, I wasn't sure what my next move would be. I sat around for a couple of days, feeling lost. The streets were very tense. The military had closed off all traffic from Fourteenth Street down. Everything was on hold, and so were all my plans. I have always believed that when one door closes, another door opens. But right then I was wondering, *Where the hell is that next door at?* Suddenly, I was practically broke, and the city was in shock. Nobody was going anywhere to get their kicks.

Work and a paycheck were not going to come easy. But I'm a survivor, and I had always managed to work something out. I needed to make something happen quick. I was paying $2,700 a month for a shoebox apartment in the East Village. Back in 2001, landlords had zero compassion and were not up for bartering rent deals. It was sink or swim. It was sketchy on the streets and hard to connect with people, too. And the city was practically shut down in response to 9/11.

After a couple weeks of laying low, with no work and no real communication, my phone rang one day. It was my boss, Michael Ault, who had started me in the nightclub business. Michael had discovered me in Miami Beach when I first moved to America a few years before. His two partners, Tony Theodore and David Sarner, dominated the NYC nightlife back in the day and pretty much created bottle service as we know it. I was always very grateful for the opportunities they gave me.

Michael said, "I'm giving serious thought to opening a space on Lafayette Street in Manhattan."

This was about a fifteen-minute walk from my apartment, and I was clean out of options. Bungalow 8 could no longer afford my door-guy services, and my door hosting job at Chaos nightclub looked like it might end as all three partners were going in different directions about what they wanted from the club. Since I had nothing else going on, I agreed to meet with Michael and his new partner, Matthew Arden.

"I found an old restaurant," Michael went on. "We're going to convert it and make it the hottest club in New York."

Michael was passionate and a go-getter, so I thought, *Why not?*

They offered me a small partnership percentage and the door job at newly opened Pangea. In sum, Pangea was a massive success, and with that success came my spiral into insanity. The pressure of the city had me by the balls. I didn't know my head from my ass. I was suddenly making a ton of money, drinking a bottle of vodka a night, snorting practically a fistful of cocaine every day, and getting into both verbal and fistfights. I was losing my mind. My ego was out of control. *I* was out of control. All of this not only ended my business partnership with Michael at Pangea—it ended my marriage, too.

After the dust settled, I opened Dorcia, a club that had a lot of potential. But with the heady combination of alcohol and cocaine, plus the addition of some bad partners, the club soon fell apart. I didn't have any real sense of purpose. I was all over the place. But, what the hell? At least I had enough money to support my drugs of choice. At the time, I thought that was all I needed.

A chance meeting on the street sent me in yet another direction. On my way home one night, I bumped into an old friend, Becky Scott, who was out with her friend, Brett Scallions, the lead singer and rhythm guitarist for Fuel. At the time, Fuel was a great rock band with a stack of hits on the charts. Brett is one of the nicest guys in the world, and we easily hit it off and became fast buddies. Fuel was in the process of writing new material after its last album had absolutely crushed it.

Reeling from the Dorcia disaster and another now-struggling restaurant venture I'd gotten into, Brett and I started brainstorming, and he came up with an idea. Again out of options, I was all ears. Brett was best friends with Duff McKagan, the former bassist with Guns N' Roses who was now in the newly formed supergroup Velvet Revolver. "I'll talk to Duff and see if he wants to get involved with a rock bar," Brett said.

Long story short, the calls were made, and I eventually hooked up with Duff and Scott Weiland, former lead singer with Stone Temple Pilots. And BOOM! The nightclub we called Snitch was born.

ROCK BOTTOM ALWAYS COMES

Being from a small town like Perth, a place that famous rock-star bands on tour often bypassed, I had always wanted to open a club where people could see the biggest bands in the world play on the smallest stage. I might have found the right space, but I also had the misfortune of once again teaming up with the wrong partner (who shall remain nameless) when I launched Snitch. This later tarnished my relationship with Brett and Duff. Scott and I, however, remained friends and even did a few TV projects together. Brett had brought Scott and Duff in as partners in name only, meaning they didn't participate in the day-to-day operation of the bar. Their names were mostly for show.

Snitch should have been a layup. Instead, it was a hot disaster, and I take full responsibility for the mess. After Scott, Duff, and Brett moved on, it didn't help that my replacement partner turned out to be one of the worst businesspeople in the world. Again, I won't name him here; I don't need to because practically everyone in NYC knows who he is.

My lack of clarity, massive ego, heavy drinking, and drug issues were a ticking time bomb. Days turned into nights, and nights turned into days in one massive blur. I had a crazy tolerance for cocaine and alcohol. I could drink and do coke all night, then go to bed, wake up the next morning, walk my dogs, and go to the gym like nothing had happened. And that was one of the main reasons why I kept doing it.

I never needed sleeping pills to come down, either. When you start drinking alcohol at age twelve and doing drugs at thirteen, substances just settle in as part of your life. My drug-and-alcohol-fueled mindset was "Work hard and play harder." I was doing eight balls of cocaine and a bottle of liquor a night like there was no tomorrow.

At the time, I thought I had the world in the palm of my hand; in reality, it was all coming undone. I was out to lunch without a menu.

By now, you're probably wondering—at what point did I actually hit rock bottom and turn my life around? If I were reading this, it would be my first question, too. Stay tuned. We're getting there, but I've got farther to fall first.

One night, I introduced tattoo artist Ami James to Charlie Chorwin, a TV producer who owned Original Media, a fast-rising production company. Charlie was looking for a tattooist for a TV series he wanted to produce called *Miami Ink*.

Charlie and I hit it off, and we teamed up to shoot a pilot for VH1 called *Dive*. What a prophetic name, right? This is where good ol' Mike Diamond destroys his life on live camera. Scott Weiland came on board and recapped some of the early insanity of our failed business partnership. (Imagine owning a bar with Scott Weiland!)

Back in 2004, *Dive* was one of the first bar reality TV shows. It tested well but was never picked up. Lucky for me that it was way before its time because otherwise my demise would have been recorded for posterity.

The night before we started shooting *Dive*, I decided to go to a party at Pink Elephant, a primo hot spot in NYC at the time. I was having a blast at this Tommy Hilfiger party, and I thought it would be a good idea to chug a bottle of vodka. Yes, an entire bottle of vodka. That's how I drank. That's the madness I was living at the time.

I was about to start dancing on the bar like a guy version of *Coyote Ugly* when my good friend Bobby, who was the owner, grabbed me by the arm. He said, "I love you, buddy, but I can't have you die in here."

I shot Bobby a look of disgust and headed for the exit. Man, I was pissed at having my fun spoiled!

It had begun to rain as I walked down Twenty-Seventh Street. I looked up the block to Bungalow 8 and spotted my good friend Armin in an argument. Armin and I had worked together at Chaos, and we always had each other's back. I trotted on over to see what was going on and if he needed my help.

Back then, I had a hair trigger and was always ready to fight. Within a split second, there we were on the street beating the shit out of three other guys. Slipping and sliding in the rain, throwing vicious punches, angry and wrestling. I felt my ankle roll, but I was still fighting—until I heard it go *pop!* Sure, it hurt like hell, but I thought nothing of it at the time. I had more ass to kick.

I would have kept going, but the fight was broken up by club security. I jumped into a cab before the police arrived. Don't ask me how, but amidst the craziness, I'd convinced some random hot babe to come home with me. To this day, I don't know who she was; I was next-level out of it.

My body somehow knew I had to be on set at 9 AM to start shooting my VH1 pilot with Scott. When I woke up at seven, I didn't feel hungover, but I just didn't feel right all the same. I just thought I was still a little tipsy and high from the night of partying. I was about to get up and walk my dogs when I looked down at my ankle and thought, *Hmmm, that doesn't look too good.* My ankle was not only swollen, but also bent, twisted, and blue.

A normal person would have headed straight to the emergency room to deal with it. Me? I had a better plan. I pulled out a bag of coke and laid out two massive lines. Here's the irony about cocaine: the more insane things get, the more you think you're in complete control of the situation. People used to say I did shoelaces of cocaine back in the day. I snorted the two whopping lines right up my nose, drank a Bloody Mary (because, you know, you *must* have your vitamins), taped up my busted ankle, walked my dogs, then headed off to the first day of shooting.

Yes, that was my reality and my insanity. Like I said, "Work hard and play harder." In those days, when anybody would tell me they lacked drive, I'd say, "Really? Shut up, get up, and go."

I didn't get to the hospital until a day later, after someone on set told one of the producers on the show about my ankle. He insisted that I needed to go.

I headed to the closest emergency room, which was only a few blocks away from where we'd been shooting. I was tired, grumpy, and hungry. I wasn't in the mood to go to the hospital, but I honestly needed some pain-killers. I hadn't had much to eat all day—just a protein bar and a turkey sandwich—and was starting to feel lightheaded and a little nauseous. Fortunately for me, the emergency room was empty. I filled in the appropriate forms and within a few minutes was greeted by a young, energetic, upbeat doctor.

She asked me why I was there. I knew I couldn't go into much detail about my last twenty-four hours, or she would probably check me into either a rehab facility or a psych ward. So I kept it simple. I told her I was a stunt man and that I'd fallen earlier in the day and twisted my ankle while we were shooting a fight scene—but that it wasn't a big deal. She asked me to remove my sock and shoe so she could take a look. When I took my sock off, my foot looked hideous and stunk. It was twisted to the left, purple, and grotesquely swollen.

"Oh, wow," she said. "That doesn't look good at all. Are you okay?"

I didn't want to show her I was in any pain, so I laughed it off and said I was fine. Honestly, I wasn't.

"We may have to get some X-rays done to really assess how bad your injury is."

Now, I didn't have time for that, as I had to shoot for the next six weeks. I had to think fast. "Look, I'm going to tell it to you straight," I said. "I'm not getting an X-ray. I have to shoot a TV show for the next six weeks, and I have to work around that schedule. If you could write me a script for some pain pills, I'll be fine."

At this point, I could see the doctor knew I was pretty jacked up and out of my mind. She kept insisting on an X-ray, and I knew it was time to bounce. I put my shoe and sock back on, headed out the door, and bee-lined it back to my apartment. I told the producers it was just a strain and nothing to worry about. Like any good addiction-fueled maniac, instead of actually addressing the problem, I woke up every morning, taped up my ankle until it felt good and encased in cement, walked my dogs (it was my responsibility, after all), did several lines of coke, and headed out for the day to shoot the show. A week after we wrapped up the shooting, I finally got my ankle looked at. I'd fractured it bad and had to wear a Moon Boot for six weeks. I'm very lucky I didn't do any permanent damage to it.

At no point during any of this did I look at my life and think I was out of control.

A MOMENT OF CLARITY IN THE CHAOS

One night after we'd wrapped up shooting *Dive*—when I'd been on a bender for weeks, snorting and drinking—I had a sober moment that changed my life forever. Scott and I were out together, and his then-wife, Mary, was calling him on his cell phone. Mary announced she was leaving Scott and taking the kids because she was sick and tired of his reckless behavior. (It's none of my business to go into lurid details about Scott or Mary. You can buy their books and let them tell their own stories.)

What should have been a defining moment for Scott became a turning point for me. I was zapped to the core as if struck by a lightning bolt.

For a moment—the first moment in a long time—I stood back and looked at my life. A guy from small-town Perth, shooting a VH1 show about his life with one of the biggest rock stars in the world. I was making a truckload of money. Doing a boatload of drugs and alcohol. In sum, I was living like a rock star myself, yet I was miserable. And I was horrendously disappointed in myself for becoming what I'd turned out to be . . . a motherf'ing addict.

Then I asked myself a simple question: "If I'm so freaking unhappy, then why the hell am I living like this?" And I questioned myself further: "What's my purpose? Where will I be in five, ten years from now? Will I even still be alive?"

After Scott took off, I sat alone that night. I knew I needed to make a change. I have never been afraid of death. But I am deathly afraid of not living at my full potential. And I knew that I was cheating myself out of that.

I called a friend who was fourteen years sober and said, "I'm done." I asked him to come get me. Minutes later, I walked into my first AA meeting and shut my mouth; from then on, I did whatever it took. And, as of April 16, 2020, as I finish writing this chapter—I, too, am fourteen years sober.

Scott and I remained friends. I had been sober for ten years when he passed away in an incredibly sad and cruel twist. I was in a rehab facility helping another friend detox on the night when Scott Weiland, my friend and one of the greatest lead vocalists of all time, died of an accidental overdose of cocaine, ethanol, and MDA.

The reality of that moment cut deep. I knew if I hadn't stopped living the way I was when I had, I would have died myself, and long before Scott. And Scott wasn't the only one. I have lost too many dear friends I couldn't reach along the way.

IF NOT *NOW* . . . WHEN?

In my first book, I went through seven simple steps to help readers remove fear and shift their mindsets. To date, *7 Steps to an Unbreakable Mindset* continues to sell very well. I have been able to help a lot of people. I do workshops, speak at high schools and conventions, cohost popular podcasts—all with the aim of helping people get on track for living their purpose in life. In *7 Steps*, I kept it simple, gave people some background on my life, and included other people's stories about how they came to make more empowering choices.

A lot has changed since then.

I feel that now it's time to give people some more tools to become the best they can be. This pandemic and the resulting economic fallout will change us forever. In times like these, it is essential to find purpose, connect to our Source for clarity and guidance, and trade a life of disempowering choices for one of empowering choices, like I did on that night in NYC fourteen years ago.

There are two important things to remember in life. Nothing is permanent in a body, and we all have an expiration date. We take nothing with us when we die. Like they say, you'll never see a U-Haul van behind a hearse at a funeral.

I often say, "Anyone can be spiritual in the feast, but what happens in the famine?" What happens when we lose everything around us? We see who people really are when they're faced with the realities of life—when they look at things head-on and face the storm. Our ability to become self-aware of how we think, feel, and act is so important in these uncertain times. Becoming emotionally intelligent gives us social intelligence and helps us synchronize with other people. And people need help and hope now more than ever.

Earlier today, I held a copy of *Recovery Today* in my hands; it's an incredible magazine about hope and spirituality. I looked at the cover and saw my own face looking back at me. Two days before my fourteen-years-sober birthday, and I had made the cover. As a kid, I wanted to one day be on the cover of *Rolling Stone*, so the comparison was not lost on me.

I can't explain how surreal it feels. Years ago, when people tried to tell me that getting sober would change my life forever, I thought they were insane. I didn't talk about my excessive drug and alcohol use in *7 Steps*. I usually saved that for AA meetings and working with clients to help them get on a fast-track for success.

But I felt now was the time to let readers in on my madness before sharing the tools I have used to turn my life around. The reality is that if I hadn't gotten sober when I did, I have no doubt whatsoever that I wouldn't be here to share this book with you. I wouldn't have lived to channel the calm and focus so many have needed in the middle of this global pandemic. I wouldn't have fallen in love with my wife, who has never seen me drink or do drugs. And I wouldn't be able to show my son how to be a leader or show others how to walk the talk.

Chapter 2

CHOOSING EMPOWERMENT

June 14, 2017, was a special day to me for two reasons. First: it was my birthday.

However, I don't really care all that much about birthdays. A lot of it has to do with my past. I seldom enjoyed my birthdays when I was younger. Growing up, there wasn't a lot of celebrating in my house. My mother couldn't cope with the extra effort involved. She'd stress out and panic at the thought of organizing any kind of birthday celebration for any one of us four kids. Therefore, my birthday was never a big deal.

Second: on this special day, my wife, Kim, had an awesome surprise for me. "We're having a baby!" she declared. However, we didn't know the sex. She sprung the good news on me right after I'd gotten home from running some errands. I had a feeling it was a girl, but I honestly wasn't set on anything so long as the baby was healthy.

This all had me in a celebratory mood, so I headed off to the gym for a workout. That's right, no champagne, no beers—just a healthy dose of endorphins.

I hadn't been feeling too well over the last couple of days. My past drinking habits were claiming their due. I presumed my ulcerative colitis was flaring up again. By now I was used to the ups and downs of the illness, though, so I thought nothing of it.

The few health issues I have today are directly linked to my drug and alcohol abuse. It's the lifetime price I will have to pay for my bad choices. I was diagnosed with ulcerative colitis back in 2010 after a getting a colonoscopy and a checkup when it became clear something wasn't right with my stomach. I constantly suffered from cramps, bloating, and gas after my meals. I always had blood in my stool and very rarely had a solid bowel movement. My nickname was Mikey Mudbutt—funny but not funny. It's not a fun disease at all. No one likes to spend their days camped out in the bathroom, and I have spent many days I'd like to forget running back and forth, sometimes soiling myself.

Every day that I train, I like to challenge myself. It's part of my ex-crackhead mindset. Maybe there is one advantage to being an addict—once we set our minds on a task, we just go for it and won't quit, no matter how hard it is.

On this day, celebrating at the gym, I thought, *Why not do a pull-up challenge?* I looked up "most weighted pull-ups in an hour" on the internet. Some crazy guy did 335 of them while wearing a forty-five-pound weighted vest. This was no easy feat, but I wanted to step up to the challenge. *Why not try and smash out three hundred in sixty minutes?* I asked myself. That's five weighted pull-ups a minute.

I wasn't feeling too hot that day but knew I could do at least two hundred. I found a forty-five-pound weight in the gym, tied it to myself with a chain, and then got started. I was pushing myself along quite well, but my stomach was kicking back viciously. Still, I pushed harder and knocked out 280 in sixty minutes.

Hey, not bad for a first run at the record, I complimented myself.

My stomach didn't exactly agree. It was pretty jacked up as I headed home.

Kim wasn't impressed when I told her over lunch about my go at setting a new record. She was always cautioning me about pushing myself too hard with my ulcerative colitis issues. Ulcerative colitis isn't a pretty picture, but I'd had it for so long, I figured I knew how to contend with it by now.

I relaxed for the rest of the day, and we went out to dinner that night. My stomach wasn't doing too good, but I ignored the pain.

We sat down at Jimmy's Steakhouse, and when I said I wasn't really hungry, Kim was shocked. I love steak and have no problem wolfing down a twenty-ounce ribeye on an average day. She had a look of surprise on her face when I ordered an eight-ounce filet—and another one when I struggled to finish it. We headed home, and I laid around like a couch potato, watching some mindless television.

My stomach was cramping up bad, but I didn't have diarrhea, which was strange. Usually with ulcerative colitis, when you're cramping up and flaring, you have the runs. Not this time.

We went to bed around 11 PM. I tossed and turned all night with insane cramps, sweating like a marathon runner, and just couldn't get comfortable. I decided to sleep on the couch so I wouldn't keep my wife up. You don't want to piss off a pregnant woman. But I was in severe pain and cramping badly. I started to wonder, *What the hell's going on?*

I sat up on the couch and was trying to breathe through the agonizing pain when Kim came downstairs. She looked at me funny and asked, "Why are you sitting on the couch?"

Trying my best to man up, I mumbled, "I didn't want to wake you, but my stomach's a wee bit off."

Classic understatement.

All of a sudden, I was hit with a cramp that felt like I'd been shot with a nine-millimeter. I hit the floor, crippled by the pain. Kim was in shock. I looked up at her and managed to whisper, "Shit, I think my appendix burst. Get me to the ER."

I was gripping my stomach with both hands but still trying to keep my cool and not freak her out. The last thing I wanted to do was stress Kim out while she was pregnant. I took a deep breath and tried to regain my composure.

But I couldn't deny the truth any longer. I knew the cramps were much more serious than my usual colitis pain. I have a massive pain tolerance, but this was way into the red zone.

Kim helped me into the car, and we hurried to the ER. I was in the back-seat and couldn't get comfortable, tossing, turning, and even screaming in excruciating pain. Every cramp felt like I was being shanked. How did I know? I was stabbed many years ago in a fight while running the door at Chaos. But this was way worse than that.

When we got to the ER, I hit the floor. I couldn't walk. The pain was off the charts. After they got me settled into a wheelchair, the nurse gave me an empathetic smile and said, "I'm not going to ask you what your pain is out of ten."

I half-smiled back and said, "Fifty."

While they were rushing me to the back, I asked, "Please give me a CT scan. I'm pretty sure my appendix burst."

The nurse looked at me, confused. "How long have you been in pain?"

"Couple days, on and off."

She said, "If your appendix had burst, trust me, you wouldn't have been able to deal with it for two days."

The nurse gave me a CT scan. Another nurse started to pump me full of painkillers. I'm not sure how much they're allowed to dose you in a hos-pital for safety reasons, but it didn't do squat to help me. I remembered doing heroin back in the day, and man, it used to knock me on my ass! This stuff was as useless as baby aspirin.

The nurse raced back in a panic, holding the CT results. She said, "Your appendix did burst, but that's not all. You are in septic shock, and your stomach is a mess of infection."

Meanwhile, back at the waiting room, Kim had called my best friend, Rob, whose birthday is the same day as mine. Rob lives in Huntington Beach, and we met in NYC many years ago when I was coked out of my mind. After getting the news from Kim, Rob did the thirty-mile drive from Huntington Beach to Glendora in a record-setting twenty-two minutes. He's a hellcat, that Rob.

I have always trusted my intuition, what I continually refer to as our Source. Rob and I had planned to go on a road trip that day to celebrate our birthdays, heading to the desert to shoot guns at bottles and tin cans. You know, just have a regular boys' day out. For some reason that I couldn't put my finger on at the time, the trip didn't feel quite right as the day grew near, so I called off the outing and stayed put in LA. If I'd gone on that trip, I wouldn't have ended up in the hospital in good care. Picture me in the desert, miles away from civilization, with a burst appendix. Not a pretty scenario, to say the least. And you probably wouldn't be reading this book—if you know what I mean. *Thank you, Source, for the guidance.*

With the CT scans revealing the horrendous news, the nurse had to find a doctor with the balls to tackle the convoluted mess my body was in. Out of nowhere, this miracle nurse located a surgeon, who drove from Barstow—an hour and a half away—to come do my surgery.

After viewing the CTs, the surgeon wasn't very optimistic, but at least he was honest. "You're in pretty bad shape, my friend," he said. Doc went on to say he was confused as to why it had taken me so long to come into the hospital, and he wondered how I'd been able to manage what must have been excruciating pain.

Easy. Growing up, I suffered a lot at the hands of my father, who'd basically used me as his punching bag. When you are abused physically (and also mentally), you learn to become resilient. But ignoring this pain like I'd done was going to come at a cost. The doctor only gave me a 50 percent chance of surviving the surgery.

I just took in the information. I had no choice but to listen. He said flatly, "Because of your ulcerative colitis, I can't save your colon. Furthermore, septic shock indicates your stomach will be a wreck."

I looked him in the eyes and said in no uncertain terms, "I *do not* want to have a bag, and I don't want you to take out my colon."

But, of course, I wasn't in any position of power, and I'm not an idiot. We came to an agreement that if saving my life meant losing my colon, then I didn't have a choice.

I was surprisingly calm, laying on the gurney. I really wasn't sure if I'd make it through the surgery. But I had full faith in my Source and knew if it was time to leave my body and go home, well, then that was that. I know nothing is permanent and that we are all connected on a higher plane. So death of the body has never worried me. It's a reality we cannot escape.

I don't focus on what I can't change—only the things I can. That's my mindset. It's a very honest and humbling experience to sit and wonder if your time is up. I had lived a very full life up to that moment, and I really started to think in the silence.

I told Kim not to worry, and she and Rob walked out together to wait. I sat and stared at the ceiling until the doctor approached me and asked me if I was okay. I looked at him and said, "Yeah. Let's do this."

He asked me if I wanted to say a prayer with him.

"I just need a moment to myself," I said.

I knew this was it. This was bigger than me, and I couldn't muscle my way through this one. It was weird; I can remember thinking that if I didn't make it through, my wife was going to be really pissed. I chuckled to myself. I know that sounds crazy, but when you are faced with the reality of a life-or-death situation, all you can do is let go and surrender to your Source. Then you just ride out the storm.

It was interesting to ponder the possibility of this being my last moment in a body. I thought about all the things that I still wanted to do in my life. I wasn't angry. Rather, I felt that I'd been rather blessed in this life.

Not being present for the birth of my first child and not seeing him grow up would suck. But at this point, it was out of my hands. I closed my eyes and had a quiet moment with my Source: "I trust you, and if I make it through the surgery, I know my life will never again be the same."

I was in surgery for three hours and thirty minutes. My insides were a disaster. The surgeon had to remove seven inches from my intestines that were riddled with infection. He left my colon intact and later told me there was no way in hell that it would heal. Sobering words for a man who was already sober.

I spent six days in the hospital. I had lost forty-five pounds and was destroyed. I could barely walk, and my mind was a mess. Bedridden, broken, and on a regimen of narcotics, I felt like pure crap. I have never been a fan of pain pills. Previously, I hadn't been on any colitis medication because the side effects were horrible. But I was now at the mercy of narcotics, and as someone who had worked so hard for sobriety, the irony didn't escape me.

Being unable to work out or move around had me twisted mentally. When I went back in for a checkup two weeks after my surgery, Doc laid it on thick: "Either I go back in and take your colon out, or you will get colon cancer and die within a year."

I knew I had to do some soul searching, as this decision was about way more than just me. Kim was nine weeks pregnant, and I was still completely destroyed from my first surgery. I knew it was up to me and my Source.

This was my new reality. I could lose my colon and likely get cancer, as I'd been told. Or I could stay on heavy doses of pain pills and colitis meds that had more bad side effects than positive results. I wasn't having it. I saw no choice but to find a natural way to heal myself.

The ripple effect of one decision can change the course of our lives forever. I had to decide whether to trust myself—that I could naturally heal my body—or to listen to Doc. I figured I'd lost enough already. It was time to knuckle down and let the rubber hit the road.

WALKING THE TALK

The road to recovery was a long, arduous one. I was flying back and forth from LA and NYC to consult on a restaurant deal that was turning into a disaster. I'd taken on way more than I expected, and it was exacting its toll on my health. I did my best to follow my doctor's orders, but despite all the work I was putting in to heal my body, I wasn't recovering correctly due to all the traveling.

I'd been in the restaurant and bar business since 1997. It was my go-to because the money was always consistent, so I took a contract to consult for a restaurant hoping it would be low stress, and easy money, and allow me to build up my coaching and speaking business that I had been working on since 2013. But things didn't turn out how I had planned, and within no time the consulting was consuming almost all of my time.

On November 21, 2017, my wife asked me to please come home for Thanksgiving. Kim has a quiet, steady presence and doesn't really complain about anything, but I could tell she needed more support through her pregnancy.

Kim and I have a great relationship. The famous sociologist Robert Francis Winch had something right when he said that opposites attract. We are completely opposite—I mean *completely* opposite—Kim values fun and having a good time. She loves food with a passion. Unlike me, who is always trying to reach the next mountaintop, Kim likes to work when she wants to, striking her perfect work–life balance, and she's built a career where she can do exactly that. Kim and I grew up in completely different environments, and it's interesting to consider the challenges and benefits of partnership between people with different backgrounds. Kim wasn't forced to overwork by her parents. She didn't have to people-please constantly to win others' affection. My upbringing conditioned me to compete, compete, compete—to overwork and grind nonstop. If it weren't for Kim, I probably wouldn't take any time off to enjoy life. It's because of her that we've traveled a lot over the years, seeing cities like Paris, Rome, Barcelona, and Florence, and even making the long trip back to Perth together. She's done so much for me, so when I could feel she was struggling with me being away, I knew it was time to head home and give her the support she needed.

I got into LAX around 7 PM on Wednesday, November 22, tired, stressed, and jet-lagged. After a late dinner around 11 PM, we hit the sack.

At 2:30 AM, Kim shook me awake and said, "I think my water broke."

I chuckled and said, "Nah. Can't be. It's too soon." No way this was happening. The due date was seven weeks away.

"I'm serious," she said in the most serious voice I'd ever heard from her.

We drove to the ER not saying much. My wife doesn't stress about anything, so we were playing it cool. Kim is incredibly grounded.

The first ER we came to, at Foothill Presbyterian Hospital in Glendora, didn't have a NICU. So we piled back into the car and drove to Queen of the Valley Hospital in West Covina. We still weren't really sure what was going on, but thankfully Kim was admitted.

The doctor ran some tests to see if her water had indeed broke, then left the exam room. Kim was sitting there, very positive and upbeat, chatting away with a nurse, hoping it'd be a false alarm and they'd send her home.

The nurse, similarly calm, said, "The plan will probably be to monitor Kim and the baby at home over the next two weeks so he'll deliver closer to his actual due date."

Everything seemed to be going smoothly—then BOOM! The doctor walked back in holding a large sheet of film and said, "Okay guys, I'll be doing an emergency C-section."

We both looked at each other. WTF?

He explained that the baby's umbilical cord was wrapping around his neck.

Orlando Diamond was born November 23, 2017, seven weeks premature. Kim was originally set on naming him Sebastian, but when I put the kibosh on that, she casually shrugged it off and said, "How about . . . Orlando?"

I immediately liked the sound of it; when I looked up the name, I found it meant "famous throughout the land."

"That sits good with me," I said with a wink.

All humor aside, I knew that I had a huge responsibility. I was a father. Talk is cheap, and now, more than ever, I had to walk the talk. To be the leader and role model I talked about being, I would have to dig deep. I hadn't moved away from Perth to repeat the cycle and be like my dad, who worked sixteen-hour days. My mother hadn't coped well with four energetic kids and very little help from him. My mum did the best she could, but with everything else going on, neither parent really connected with me. My younger sister was born thirteen weeks premature in 1978, way before neonatal care was as advanced as it is today. My older brother contracted measles encephalitis at seven and wound up in a coma. He was never the same again. I got lost somewhere in the shuffle of all of that. My younger brother was the golden child. Me? I was just naughty Mike-in-the-middle who needed a good belting.

I wanted to be the dad to my child that I didn't have. But here I was, still trying to recover from my stomach surgery, still trying to naturally heal my colon to avoid a second surgery or worse, and knowing that if I didn't go back to New York, the restaurant that I'd just opened would implode for sure.

I sat in meditation and asked my Source for the answer. I had to find a way to stay in LA full-time. Be a dad. Stay sober. Coach. Do workshops and publish my first book. Coaching and motivational speaking without the luxury of my steady restaurant-consulting gravy was going to be tough, but I had to find a way. It was time to say a permanent goodbye to the service business and start serving people in other ways.

I called a friend, Matt, who worked in the mental health industry. When I'm trying to find an opportunity, I always make a ton of calls and take massive action to create a change. I feel that's where people get stuck. Fear can either motivate us or keep us frozen. Like they say: fight, flight, or freeze. You have to make the choice to fight, to act, to get on the phone.

Matt said he and his brother had opened a lockdown facility for teens near Death Valley in Nevada. Matt asked me if I would be interested in working with the kids at the facility on a one-to-one basis. I'd be teaching the kids how to set goals, exercise, and meditate. It was all exactly up my alley.

The problem: it was a four-hour drive from home. I asked Kim, "You okay with me working three days a week out of town?"

"As long as the town isn't New York," she grinned, "yeah, I can manage."

And as fortune would have it, Kim's parents lived down the street and were more than willing to help us out.

The Never Give Up Youth Healing Center was created by Matt and Daniel Cox. Its mission and purpose were to help young kids who were clashing with their parents, falling behind at school, and getting in trouble with the law. Some of the kids came from broken homes, the foster care system, and juvenile detention facilities.

The facility was equipped to house up to sixty kids at one time and had a full treatment staff, cleaning staff, chef, and full gymnasium for the kids to let off steam. It was a well-organized and highly structured environment that sought to teach kids better habits for success while processing their past trauma.

Despite the modest pay, I took the job. I would wake the kids up at the crack of dawn, which none of them liked. First thing on the agenda was to make their beds, like in the military. Then they had to journal their thoughts for ten minutes. After that, they had to have a cold shower, which they also hated. From there, we would go to the gymnasium to exercise. I kept things very simple and straightforward: stretching, running, and calisthenics. We would end with a simple ten-minute mindfulness meditation. I would then walk the kids back to the dorms so they could get dressed and ready for breakfast and class. We also worked on meditation practices, and I supported them in processing the invalidating feelings they had carried for too long. I kept the routine very structured and simple in the hopes of teaching them how to make more empowering choices and develop better habits.

It was also great for me as well. Whenever I coach someone, I do the work with them. Teaching people helps reaffirm the actions we, too, need to take to be successful. At the Center, I found a path into the true work I wanted to do and felt grounded.

The truth was that I was burned out from trying to take shortcuts to make it big. The Center gave me the place to test and further develop the principles I was writing about, speaking about, and coaching others on. In my coaching work, I always tell others, "We all have the ability to reach our full potential in life if we put ourselves to the test." Now it was my turn to walk the talk I was constantly dishing out.

I created a ninety-day program based on mindfulness principles I'd studied. The purpose was to help these troubled teens break bad habits and make more empowering choices. I based the course on the book I was writing.

The kids and I got along great. Having been a troublesome teen myself, I could easily identify with them. And I knew the importance of having good role models. Most kids who end up getting kicked out of school, like I did, and get in trouble with the law are just crying out for attention. We all need love and support. I do not remember a time growing up when I felt any real love from my parents. There was too much going on in my house, with my older brother needing rehabilitation therapy and my father always working. I don't blame anyone for my drug addiction or struggles . . . in fact, it's all part of what has made me who I am today. But I do know one thing: without love and good role models, we tend to make disempowering choices.

As I said earlier, I started drinking at twelve. My dad owned liquor stores, and there was booze stored all over our house. It was easy for me to get my hands on it without ever being busted. Cannabis came next, and I got caught and expelled from an exclusive private school, Aquinas College, for dealing.

The fallout was catastrophic. My dad went ballistic. I was a marked man, and it didn't matter what I did from then on because I had already shamed the family. The black-sheep dynamics had been there for years, but now there was proof I was no good. That's why I could connect with these teens. I was one of them; I had been there, too: disempowered and unsupported by those who were supposed to hold me up.

After working at the facility for six months I decided to move on and focus my attention on one-on-one coaching. The owners and I parted ways on good terms, and the experience really helped me refine my skills as a coach. At this point in time, I had just self-published 7 *Steps to an Unbreakable Mindset*, and it was producing good numbers. Still, I needed more income, and the universe smiled on me once again. One afternoon, as I was getting ready to leave the lockdown for the last time, I bumped into my neighbor, who was also named Matt. He asked me, "How's it going with the teens?"

"It was amazing," I replied. "I loved doing it, but now I have to move on."

Matt paused to think for a moment, then asked me, "Do you have any interest in speaking at high schools?

My ears perked up like a terrier's. "Y-yes . . . are you psychic? How did you know I'm trying to become a full-time speaker?"

Matt went on to tell me about his friend Al, who owned a company called Impact Canine Solutions. Al provided K-9 dogs to high schools to help control the use of drugs, nicotine, and alcohol on school campuses across LA County.

The next day, Matt introduced me to Al Hradecky. "There's an opportunity for us to speak all throughout LA County," Al explained.

It sounded too good to be true, so I asked, "What's the hitch?"

"Well," he said tentatively, "we'll need to create an anti-vaping program."

I was honest and said, "I'll need to do some homework." Al figured that was a "maybe"—until I grinned and said, "But I'm all in."

Al and I worked furiously to create a sixty-minute PowerPoint covering the effects of vaping, drugs, and alcohol on the adolescent mind. Al also gave me the green light to sell my books and add in my own story of drug and alcohol abuse to help inspire the kids to make better choices.

All told, Al and I did more than 150 talks in twelve months. The program, called Impacted Youth, still runs today. At the same time, I had parlayed doing workshops with car dealerships and insurance companies such as Aflac and State Farm, helping their employees to manage stress and set more empowering goals, into a burgeoning coaching and speaking business, just as I'd dreamed. I still showed up to work every day to speak at high schools and conventions. But by then I was also doing private coaching for an ever-lengthening list of clients.

The only problem . . . I was still healing very slowly.

I knew I needed to find a way to push myself and my body into believing I could heal. I was flicking through documentaries on YouTube, looking for inspiration, when Dean Karnazes's TED Talk popped up. Dean's story is amazing! Please look it up. On his thirtieth birthday, while out drinking with his friends, he suddenly decided he needed a change in his life. Dean left the bar, then ran thirty miles through the night with zero training beforehand. I then binge-watched videos of other ultra runners and found myself wondering, *What would it be like to not only run a half-marathon, but to also do it while pushing Orlando in a stroller?*

As a kid, I had been a strong sprinter and even won a bunch of medals. It saddens me to remember that my dad never took one Saturday afternoon off to watch me run. And my mum would call me a show-off for winning. I couldn't catch a break at home! Back then, I knew I had the physical strength and the body of an athlete, yet I couldn't stop self-sabotaging with drugs and alcohol.

I'd heard it said: "Run a marathon, and it will change your life forever." And so, at age forty-five, I decided to enter my first half-marathon and indeed ran the race while pushing Orlando.

Twelve months later, I decided to run thirty half-marathons in thirty days to raise awareness and money to help with treatment for Layla, a little girl who suffered from a rare autoimmune disease that was so deadly, a simple cold could kill her. You'd think ulcerative colitis and the complications from a burst-appendix surgery would be enough of a handicap, right? Well, I also developed a hernia. But in the heat of an LA summer in August 2019, while most days wearing an adult diaper, I did it: I ran thirty half-marathons in thirty days, breaking a Guinness World Record along the way.

It was a very surreal and life-changing experience. I had plenty of bad days, but I didn't quit. Not once. I got up at 4 AM every morning (something I still do today) to meditate and then went for a run. At 6 AM, I went to work with my private clients and the companies I regularly consult with.

Oh, and what about Mikey's big health issue? you might be wondering. Well, after years of wanting to prove wrong the experts who said I couldn't self-heal, I decided it was time to put the same kind of energy I'd put into my running training into healing myself.

I began using intense breathwork made famous by Wim Hof, an extraordinary human who holds multiple world records for pushing himself to the limit. I ate a clean, high-protein, low-carb diet with a range of healthy fats: a ketogenic–paleo hybrid. I took a complement of high-quality vitamins, including C, D, and B, plus other supplements. I combined that with a heavy DOSE of positivity. Despite my "fatal" diagnosis, here I am today—going strong, speaking to large audiences more than two hundred times a year, sharing my story with you, and waiting to see how you'll bring it at game time and take control of your own potential.

When I work with companies or individuals, my focus is on them: How can I help them grow and expand? I have taken companies who were struggling to motivate sales teams all the way to breaking sales records. I've helped hard-core addicts walk away from drugs and alcohol and run marathons instead. I've coached single parents on how to start their own businesses. And finally, the accomplishment I'm most proud of: I taught myself to live at my full potential every day.

REACHING *YOUR* POTENTIAL

Well, readers, as you've observed over these past two chapters, everything I've done, I've done the hard way. I've shared many of my missteps and mistakes in hopes that you'll have fewer. As we move into the next part of the book, I'm going to give you my crash course to reaching your full potential.

But what is potential? And can anyone reach their full potential in life?

I heard the word "potential" bandied about all the time while I was growing up—mostly in terms of athletic ability, as in: "Will they live up to their potential as a [insert sport] player?" But even though I myself participated in athletics, I never thought about potential in terms of pursuing a pro career. And not at all regarding my personal life or career.

So I never gave potential much thought until I read the work of American psychologist Abraham Maslow, famous for his "hierarchy of needs" that culminates in self-actualization. The online dictionary Lexico defines self-actualization as: "The realization or fulfillment of one's talents and potentialities, especially considered as a drive or need present in everyone." I especially appreciate the "present in everyone" part.

Self-actualization is the quest to achieve our full potential as human beings. It comes out of the desire for self-fulfillment and the desire to be the best that we can be. Some people use the terms "self-realization" or "spiritual enlightenment." For me, the label doesn't matter all that much. It's the same process approached with similar mindsets, and it starts with an intense look at our life up until the present moment: where we are right now because of the choices we have made and where we're going tomorrow based on the choices we now make.

In 1943, Maslow wrote a paper titled "A Theory of Human Motivation." He believed that only 3 percent of people become fully self-actualized in life. Maybe that figure was accurate in '43. Today, I believe the percentage is way lower. I also believe that anyone who's willing to do the work can live at their full potential, especially now with all the tools and information for change that we have at our fingertips. Once you get help finding those resources, it comes down to simply *wanting* to and being *willing* to do the work.

As people, we tend to either make empowering or disempowering choices. I tried to take a few shortcuts over the years to reach my dreams, and I paid the price for doing so. At the Death Valley lockdown, helping teens find purpose and potential was a real challenge—but at the same time, it was one of the most rewarding things I have ever done. I actually got to witness kids who were considered hopeless, kids who were looked upon as the dregs of society, turn their lives around and move toward becoming productive, empowered citizens—people who mattered, people who would later be making a difference in the world.

EVERYTHING IS A CHOICE

As you will see through the rest of the book, I'm a big fan of acronyms. For me, they serve as mnemonics that make it easier to download and later recall helpful information.

I believe that failing is a conscious process, like any other process in life.

We FAIL when we get:

F – Frustrated, which leads to
A – Anger, which then leads to
I – Insecurity, which makes us
L – Lack perseverance.

We self-actualize, however, by asking questions that not only help us grow but also help us reach higher levels of being. Questions that help us reflect on who we are so that we can let go of the negative, embrace the positive aspects of ourselves and our experience as human beings, and develop the resiliency to avoid frustration, which starts the failure cycle.

When I first got sober, I started to really look at how people around me were feeling. It's a sad fact that a lot of people, even in sobriety, suffer from depression, anxiety, and other crippling mental health issues. I have never taken antidepressants, but I was shocked to find out how many people use them.

After my stomach surgery, I was a mess. My depression levels were hard-core. I knew that if I didn't find natural ways to reach equilibrium, I'd be in deep trouble. I could see the possibility of a relapse staring me right in my face, a return to my old disastrous coping mechanisms if I didn't take charge of my emotions and address what I was feeling in the present moment. When we are in pain, especially chronic pain, it's very easy for us to start feeling sorry for ourselves and throw in the towel. I knew I could not allow myself to think that way, as relapsing or taking a shortcut in my healing journey wasn't an option.

Today, I feel no need whatsoever to drink or do cocaine. I've learned all the lessons I had to from those chemicals. Knowing when a behavior of any kind is no longer contributing to your personal growth and identifying that you're still engaging in it out of mindless habit is an essential first step to reaching your potential. For example, I know a few people in the music industry who used marijuana to help "inspire" them to write songs. Then, one day, the well went dry, and no amount of weed would spark creativity. Yet they continued their smoking habit instead of looking for other natural ways of spurring creativity.

Being congruous and living in harmony with light and love takes a good deal of spiritual discipline. But who says maintaining a spiritual discipline can't be fun? I'm sure having the time of my life these days. If I'm not continually doing my spiritual work and connecting to my Source, though, I will act out and sink into negative headspaces. It's important to remember that you're always only one choice away from a different life, and I want to help you embrace change without having to go through all the pain I've shared.

During my recovery, I started to take a close look at my mindset and moods along with my motivation and thoughts. Through my reflection and coaching work, I've found nine areas (or tenets) where we can focus on change to find success and reach our true potential.

While this process takes work, who says work equals drudgery? When you love what you're doing, you barely notice it's actually work. For example, I love running marathons. And for me, the heavy training is just as much fun and exhilarating as crossing the finish line or even winning the race.

In the coming chapters, I will break each of the nine ingredients down for you. This is a process best described by the oxymoronic phrase "Expand and simplify."

1. Reframe your **PERSPECTIVE** in the present moment to make empowering choices.
2. Maintain a **POSITIVE** outlook on life and understand how to get a natural DOSE of positivity.
3. Live with **PURPOSE** and work with the spiritual laws of the universe.
4. Have **PRIORITIES, VALUES, and RULES** to live by so you can keep living out your purpose and potential.

5. **PERSEVERE** through continual self-improvement and advancement of your goals.
6. Practice **PATIENCE** to ride out the storm when things aren't going your way.
7. Surround yourself with the right **PEOPLE** to drive you, not disempower you.
8. Make sure you are in the right **PLACES** at the right times and equipped to best manage your time while you're there.
9. Create a multifaceted **MASTER PLAN** to create the future you dream about and begin to live it.

But that's not all, folks! I promise you plenty of other treats along the way.

Are you ready to change your life? And, for some of you, to save your life?

Like I told the doc all those years ago when my fate seemed to hang in uncertainty, "Let's do this!"

PART TWO

PART TWO

Chapter 3

REFRAME YOUR PERSPECTIVE

am always suspicious when people say they lack motivation. I think lacking motivation isn't the whole truth. As human beings, we are motivated in two simple ways: to gain pleasure and to avoid pain. So when the alarm goes off at 4, 5, or 6 AM and you hit the snooze button, you aren't unmotivated. You're just enjoying the pleasure and comfort of the cozy bed over getting up, taking a shower, and doing a meditation.

However, if you learn to associate *not* achieving your goals with pain, then guess what? You will get your ass up early and go. I know life is short. I don't waste a second of it on things that have no value for me. I'm grateful to be alive and for the life I've been graciously given.

Whenever we feel stuck, or in any situation where we wish to initiate change, we need to expand our map and shift our view of the world around us. By "map," I mean our outlook on the world. The world we see is only based on our perception and not on reality. We can change our viewpoint by gathering more information and shifting or reframing our perception, which then alters our perspective. It's important to look at our map of reality and ask ourselves, "Does this map need to be expanded?" And, if so, "Can I expand it?" Then, "How do I expand it?"

We all suffer hardships or setbacks, but how we deal with them makes all the difference. When we face adversity, becoming flexible in our mindset will help us shift. Gaining perception expands our map so we can get unstuck and expand our opportunities.

THE MINDSET FOR SUCCESS: FIXED VERSUS FLEXIBLE

Growing up, I was often told I was a loser and couldn't achieve anything. I was branded as stupid, and people would say to me, "You won't amount to anything." This was because I got poor grades in school. It wasn't until years later that my dyslexia was discovered. Hence, as a kid, reading and comprehension were a big challenge to me.

The people I grew up with based everything in life on IQ and getting good grades in school. Things like common sense and street smarts were never factored in. You were put in a box, and that was that. Fortunately for me, all my life I've been acutely aware that I have a guiding force—my intuition—even before I knew what to call it.

After I had stomach surgery, I knew that if I wanted any chance to heal myself, I'd have to expand my mindset and be willing to learn a lot of new things to naturally nurse my way back to health. The things I've learned have changed and may even have saved my life. But I never would have learned these things without first having a flexible mindset.

People with fixed mindsets believe their basic qualities, such as their intelligence or talent, are static traits that forever exist as they currently are. They spend their time documenting their intelligence or talent instead of developing them. They also believe that talent alone creates success. When I became aware that most of the doctors who were diagnosing me had fixed mindsets, I knew it was up to me to open myself up to possibilities that they couldn't even imagine. I mean, how could they? With a fixed mindset, they saw healing only one way: through prescription drugs.

I was told ulcerative colitis was genetic, as was my drug addiction. I'd been dealt a bad hand of cards, and that was all I had to play with. But my intuition informed me that I could heal myself if I stayed open and flexible to other possibilities.

People who have a flexible mindset know that by applying dedication and hard work to any task, they'll achieve their goal. They have the will to learn whatever skills it takes. These people learn to bend, not break.

It is important to understand that life will never go according to the plan we have laid out. Life is unpredictable; unexpected things happen. I think John Lennon said it best: "Life is what happens to you while you're busy making other plans."

I was first inspired by a real-life example of this true flexibility while watching palm trees bending and not breaking during a Category 5 hurricane in Miami, where I managed my first nightclub. Applying flexibility to our mindset will help us weather any storm, including the unpredictability of this global pandemic and all the uncertainties to come in its wake.

Teddy Atlas, the trainer and commentator, has a saying that he uses to inspire his fighters when they face adversity: "The fire is coming. Are you ready? Are you a firefighter?"

With a flexible mindset, you'll be able to manage your thoughts and emotions effectively and not react in fear when unforeseen circumstances come your way in life.

We need to become emotionally intelligent and take nothing personally. In my first book, I wrote about our ability to manage our fears and stay out of our sympathetic nervous system (fight, flight, or freeze mode). Our sympathetic nervous system is primed to respond to threats. When we sense danger, blood rushes to our hands, preparing us to defend ourselves (fight), and to our legs, preparing us to run from danger (flight). In some cases, we can be so overwhelmed, we just lock up—we become completely paralyzed and can't do anything (freeze). By using the STOP method detailed below, we can manage our reactions and get back into the "rest and digest" state of the parasympathetic nervous system.

When we are in the state of rest and digest, we are calm and in control of our emotions. When we are relaxed instead of in panic mode, we can think clearly and effectively process information, which aids us in keeping a flexible mindset.

Here's how STOP works. Let's say you find yourself in some kind of a crisis, and you're starting to panic—perhaps even starting to hyperventilate. Now . . .

STOP — Yes, Simply Stop

S – Stop whatever you are doing.

> Whenever you feel disturbed or triggered by someone or something and feel like you might say or do something you shouldn't (and will regret later), *stop*. Command yourself to stop whatever you're doing. I use this technique with my clients all the time, and I use it myself when I feel like my emotions are mastering me instead of the other way around. Actually telling ourselves to STOP helps ground us in the present moment.

T – Take a breath.

> I suggest taking five to ten slow, deep breaths. If you've ever watched a boxing match or UFC fight, you might have noticed that the trainers will always tell the fighters to breathe as soon as the round is finished and they return to their corner.
>
> When we sense danger, our body responds accordingly to protect us. We go into fight-or-flight mode. The parasympathetic nervous system yields to our sympathetic nervous system, blood rushes to our hands and feet, and we become ready for action. The only way to control our nervous system is through deep diaphragmatic breathing.
>
> When we are in our rest and digest state, we can operate out of our prefrontal cortex, where we make all our executive decisions. When we are in fight-or-flight mode, we operate out of our prehistoric lizard brains and only react to the immediate danger. That's why we don't make good decisions when we are charged with emotions, whether anger or fear. So just remember to breathe!

O – Observe the disturbance.

Some combination of four things is happening when you are in fight, flight, or freeze mode:

1. You're afraid you're not going to get what you want.
2. You're fearful that you might lose what you've already got.
3. You're afraid of the future.
4. You have guilt and shame for something you've done in the past.

Whenever we are in any of those four mindsets, we're not in the present moment. Living in the present moment is very important for being in control of our choices and having a sense of happiness and freedom. When we are fully present and engaged in what we are doing in real time, we don't obsess about the future—which is unknown—or ruminate over the past and things we can't change.

The following are a few suggestions to help you stay present.

Whenever you feel worried about losing an opportunity in the present moment, ask yourself this: "Is this a life-or-death situation? How important is the opportunity, really?" A lot of the time, we place heavy value on things that ultimately aren't that important but that initially feel essential to our welfare or happiness. There will always be other opportunities if we are willing to work and wait for them.

For example, if you get laid off, thinking that you've just lost the only job you'll ever have will put you at an extreme disadvantage. There's always another opportunity just around the corner if we remain open to the possibility rather than having a defeatist attitude. Whenever I get caught up in what I call "future-tripping," I slow down and take things day by day. I focus on what's important in the moment. I have found that if I am continually working on my skills and bringing value to other people, the work always materializes seemingly out of the blue.

A few years back, a tenant in my house in Las Vegas burned down my laundry room. Apparently, she didn't know the importance of taking the lint out of the dryer. I was in Australia at the time, shooting a TV show. I didn't panic. I didn't scream and yell and pull my hair out. I simply accepted that for some reason unbeknownst to me, this was supposed to happen. I found a listing and called a Vegas handyman. He took care of everything for me. And in the end, it actually worked in my favor. At a minimal cost, he repaired some other things in my house that he noticed were in dire need of fixing.

The lesson I learned was that the key to finding solutions to our day-to-day problems is to process the information calmly in the present moment and not take things personally. And avoid the guilt and shame traps. When I got sober, I had a lot of guilt and shame for some of my past behavior. I went to my sponsor for advice. He told me that the best way to remove that guilt and shame was to make amends to those toward whom I'd acted inappropriately. I know it seems crazy, but it worked. I was worried, but not one person reacted negatively. I have made many amends over the years, and doing so has not only helped me heal—it has also brightened the days of the people I had previously harmed. And it turned some of my "enemies" into good friends!

Try using some of these suggestions when you find yourself feeling overwhelmed. They have worked wonders for me.

P – Proceed.

Once we've stopped, taken a moment to breathe, and observed what has been disturbing us, we should now be in rest and digest, back in control of our emotions. From here, we should be able to make more empowering choices. We won't be *reacting* to the world around us; we will be *responding* to it.

Unfortunately, most people spend too little time in rest and digest. We are constantly bombarded by stimuli that keep us on edge. We're a society that reacts and consumes, always looking for quick fixes to feel better.

When you're in a constant state of fear (or frustration, or agitation, or anger), you cannot heal or be productive.

The STOP technique can be used when we are triggered by something in the environment and our primitive brains take over to protect us.

When we act on a feeling and don't take time to think it through, we are in danger of not processing that feeling, and as a result, our emotions can hijack us. In some cases, people act on raw emotions and later regret what they've said or done. Acting out when we are angry or resentful does not serve us. I know this all too well from the early years of getting into confrontations with people and then regretting what I said (usually a threat) or did (usually a fistfight) afterwards.

But how can we better navigate the disastrous habit of acting from a place of *feeling* rather than from a place of *thinking*? Consider my STAMP technique, which I created to help people manage their thoughts and halt the ripple effect of one negative thought after another. STAMP will help you manage your thinking to prevent you from continually ruminating on the negative, which is what causes us to stay in emergency mode, never reach a state of rest, and stay stuck in a fixed mindset.

STAMP

S - Stop what you are doing right away.

T - Take a breath, like in the STOP technique, to get out of fight, flight, or freeze mode.

A - Adjust your thinking. We can only have one thought at a time. When you adjust your thinking, it stops the ripple effect of the negative thought loop. I do this when observing my disempowering thoughts. It's just information. Be curious about the information and take nothing personally.

M - Make the change from disempowering to empowering. Find things to be grateful for in the present moment. This will shift you out of a negative thought loop that could trigger a cascade of disempowering emotions.

A few years back, I was stopped at a traffic light on my way to a speaking gig when I got rear-ended. My initial response was to go straight into fight mode. I was so pissed off that the guy hit me. I signaled to the other driver to follow me and pulled around the corner. My mind was racing a million miles an hour knowing I was going to be late for my speaking engagement. For a split second, I seriously wanted to punch the guy in the face, which always used to be my first response, unfortunately. But now I know that never ends well. I consciously started breathing—yes, breathing. I know my anger, and it's horrible if I feed it.

I sat in the car and kept breathing deeply to gain control of my thoughts and emotions. I wasn't hurt; I was just shocked from the impact. My mind started to slow down. I thought to myself, *I'm okay, and I have insurance.* I was grateful that I had a nice car (with just a little rear bumper damage) and that it was another beautiful sunny day in LA—and that in a few minutes, I was going to keynote in front of a thousand people.

I got out of the car and noticed the other driver was freaking out. I remained calm, which caused him to relax, too. We exchanged information without making a scene, and then I continued on my merry way.

I hit the stage right on time, and my presentation went smoothly. At the end, I even got a standing O. But I know that if I'd chosen to react in anger and ruminate on the incident, my speaking gig would have been a disaster.

It's taken me years to accept that life will test me constantly and that it's my responsibility to stay present and calm. The last thing I want to do is be grateful when life deals me a crappy hand. It's easy to play the victim, but it gets you nowhere. Be grateful. It works every time.

P – Proceed, now that you are back in control, to make a better choice.

When we are flexible, we become greater than our environment.

Russian physiologist Ivan Pavlov set up a famous experiment many years ago with his dogs that became a groundbreaking discovery of how we can be conditioned to respond a certain way to particular triggers in our environment. Pavlov's experiment was very simple. He'd noticed that his dogs would salivate when presented with food. So at the same time every day, before feeding his dogs, Pavlov would ring a bell. The bell became the stimulus (or trigger) for the dogs' mealtime. Eventually, the dogs started to drool in response to the bell itself in anticipation of the food associated with the stimulus.

This idea of classical conditioning has opened up a lot of discussion in the world of therapy about the importance of unconscious triggers in human behavior. For our purposes, however, Pavlov's work illustrates the effects of a fixed mindset. A flexible mindset, on the other hand, allows us to recognize or anticipate our triggers and thereby minimize or even avert their effect on us.

When we stay flexible, we don't behave like Pavlov's dogs. There are five benefits of becoming more flexible in your mindset and perspective.

1. YOU LEARN TO PERSEVERE

"You aren't going to find anybody that's going to be successful without making a sacrifice and without perseverance."
Lou Holtz

Leaning to persevere takes practice, like anything else in life. If we can learn to see setbacks and obstacles as opportunities to learn, grow, expand ourselves, and live outside our comfort zones, we will always prosper. Thinking like this allows us to create solutions to our problems and not feel stuck.

Or, as is often the case, the problem will solve itself. That is, you suddenly realize that there is no longer a problem. It mysteriously just went away after you removed the charge it had on you.

Someone who practices the art of being flexible in their thinking takes on life and enjoys playing the cards they are dealt, both good and bad.

Flexibility allows us to stay on track even when the going gets hard. It helps us continue pushing or advancing until we reach our goal. This mindset opens us up to more opportunities for success. With flexibility, life becomes a fun ride, and we can enjoy every moment of it.

2. YOU EMBRACE UNCERTAINTY AND CHANGE

"I've come to believe that all my past failure and frustration
were actually laying the foundation for the understandings
that have created the new level of living I now enjoy."
Tony Robbins

We must learn to stop fearing change by embracing the fact that change will always happen, no matter who we are or where we are in the world. Nothing remains constant. We can never go back in time, and even if we revisit someplace where we once spent time, we won't be the same as before, and neither will the place we visit.

This is why it is so important to develop a flexible mindset. Change is going to happen whether we like it or not; it's just an inevitable fact of life. It's something we must embrace and be okay with if we want to be successful and live to our full potential. One way I have learned to deal with change is by getting comfortable with adversity and the unknown mysteries of this ever-changing world we live in. Once I understood that it was okay for me to make mistakes, come up short, and not be perfect in life, I no longer carried around the limited belief that if I failed in my attempt to complete a task, then I was a failure, no good, and a loser.

Once we practice being flexible in our mindsets, we can turn a bad situation to our advantage by changing our approach and focusing on how to grow instead of moaning about why something is happening to us.

3. YOU PRACTICE ACTIVE LISTENING

"Most people do not listen with the intent to understand;
they listen with the intent to reply."
Stephen R. Covey

One of the hardest things for all of us to do is to accept each other. Anyone who says that it's easy to do is better than I am. Once I began to practice being more flexible in my mindset, I started to take the time to respect other people's perspectives. When we see the world the way someone else sees it, we instantly become more compassionate and empathetic, whether we're aware of it or not.

And connecting with others in this way truly makes us emotionally intelligent. When we become aware of our own emotions, we are more easily made aware of other people's emotions, and we understand that we are all doing the best we can with the information we have. True emotional intelligence is having the ability to accept people for who they are and not trying to dominate or control people with our own views and opinions. With active listening techniques, we become flexible and able to synchronize with other people no matter what they think, how they feel, or how they act.

There are four perceptual positions we can take that allow us to raise our self-awareness and emotional intelligence, as well as to see the world from someone else's point of view.

When we are in the first position (self), we view the world around us through our own eyes, perspective, experiences, and maps of reality. In first position, we use our five senses to orient ourselves.

In the second perceptual position (others), we take the time to try to experience life in someone else's shoes, seeing and feeling the world through their eyes. We can't visit second position if we hold any prejudices, judgments, or resentments toward the person. Putting in the effort to look at the world the way someone else does is a true sign of being empathetic.

Taking on the third position (observer) is very valuable. If you're in a discussion or debate with another person and can't seem to find some common ground, adopting the third position can be extremely useful. By taking on the role of observer, we use a more objective lens to zoom out and look at both ourselves and the person we are dealing with. This helps us better sync with others.

The fourth position (witness) isn't used often, but it's a very powerful perceptual position to practice and cultivate. When we take on this position, we take on everything before us with a very open mind. We place no judgement on what's going on. It's a very Zen-like position, and some people refer to it as being in a neutral position. We can only do this when we have zero to no emotional investment in what's happening: it's not good or bad—it just simply is what it is.

4. YOU LOOK FOR OPPORTUNITIES

"In the middle of difficulty lies opportunity."
Albert Einstein

If we learn to roll with the punches and go with the flow, we don't get stuck, bogged down, or overwhelmed when life doesn't go as we may have initially planned. When we adopt this kind of mindset, we see there are always multiple ways to handle situations. We get used to asking powerful and helpful questions, and asking such questions is a key ingredient to becoming successful. When people are stuck in dated ways of thinking and old paradigms, they never see opportunities that may be sitting right in front of them. I learned many years ago to look at everything as a lesson. Once I stopped blaming the world and the people around me when things didn't go my way, I suddenly saw opportunities everywhere.

If ever there was a good time to take action, it would be in the middle of a global pandemic. Get off the couch; stop binge-watching mindless television shows. Start coming up with new ways to educate yourself and expand your horizons.

5. YOU ARE NOT LOCKED INTO ONE ROLE

"There's no talent here. This is hard work. This is an obsession."
Conor McGregor

People who reach their full potential, achieve their goals, and find their purpose understand that they must cultivate a flexible mindset, stretch themselves, and know that life is never a static affair. The magic of life is that it's unpredictable, uncertain, and full of surprises. When we are willing to accept that, we see opportunities to learn, prosper, shine, and grow.

When I first got sober, I had to surrender to my Source. I knew I was spiritually ill and had lost my way. The more I looked into myself, at the erroneous thoughts and poor choices that got me here, the more I knew I needed to weed my thinking in order to flourish.

TEN WAYS TO KEEP US FLEXIBLE

Changing any set of behaviors or beliefs and embracing a flexible mindset requires us to practice and use different strategies. Are you ready to develop and maintain a flexible mindset? Fantastic! Below are ten techniques you can adopt in your quest for flexibility in your perspective on life.

1. GET COMFORTABLE WITH THE MYSTERY OF LIFE

Before we can develop a flexible mindset or start being more flexible, we must first get rid of any rigidity in our thinking. Fixed-mindset habits only hold us back. This new way of thinking and seeing the world must come from a growth-mindset foundation in which we get comfortable with unknown outcomes and see every obstacle as an opportunity.

Whenever we start something new, it's natural for us to fear the unknown. But you must stop thinking of things in terms of setbacks and instead start considering what you could learn. Instead of the negative excuses that generally come with a challenge, ask yourself, "Why not?" What's the worst that can happen by taking a new risk or trying something different?

Instead of letting doubt or fear stop you from moving forward, embrace the unknown, learn to take risks, and challenge yourself. By having faith in the process, we can surprise ourselves with what we can achieve.

2. LET GO OF OLD BEHAVIORS AND WAYS OF THINKING

We are all creatures of habit. We become our routines, day in and day out. The only way to change a behavior is to take action and make small incremental changes. By building a new habit, we fire new neural pathways.

I remember how lazy I was for years and how little things like making my bed seemed pointless. Then I watched a documentary on Navy SEAL training. One segment focused on the importance of making your bed. Starting the day with making your bed may seem insignificant, but it can keep you on track for success throughout the day. I added in the SEALs' regimen of taking cold morning showers as well. At first, I honestly thought it was a joke and didn't think it really had any significant meaning. *It's just a cold shower*, I thought. But then I remembered hearing someone say "What we don't like in the cold morning shower, is what we are trying to avoid in life." As crazy as it sounds, I find it true. Just as the cold showers are uncomfortable, so too can life be uncomfortable when things don't go as planned. It's now my habit to make my bed when I wake up in the morning and then take a cold shower every day, no matter how I feel, as it helps me stay on track and focused.

The next time you find yourself embarking on an old, tired routine or saying, "Well, this isn't how I always do it," switch things up! I'm not saying *you* must take a cold shower every morning to be successful. I'm simply encouraging you to try something new from time to time. Accomplish some of your everyday tasks in new and different ways.

3. LEARN THAT OBSTACLES CAN BE OPPORTUNITIES

Life, as it travels from moment to moment, is always going to be uncertain. People who believe they can predict the future are sadly mistaken and completely delusional. Now, I know that sounds a little harsh, but it's the truth. We can never predict the future—only plan for it. And even the best-prepared plans can fall apart and need adjusting. We have to look at any bumps in the road as opportunities for us to slow down and reassess our plans and strategies. When you encounter an obstacle (for instance, someone else is given the promotion you felt you deserved), take a step back. Ask yourself, "What's the lesson in this situation? What can I learn?" Gaining perspective on and distance from how you feel about something will help you see more clearly.

4. REFRAIN FROM NEGATIVE SELF-TALK AND PUT-DOWNS

The way we talk to ourselves has a huge effect on how we feel and act. Over the years, I've beat myself up constantly. I've talked down to myself when

I made mistakes. But doing so only made me make more mistakes and left me feeling miserable. We must develop an awareness of how we talk to ourselves when we make mistakes or face setbacks in life.

When I catch myself ruminating over my past failures, I say "cancel" out loud. Using this verbal cue helps me stop beating myself up. After stopping the negative talk, I then take a moment to practice positive reinforcement with myself. When we praise instead of criticize ourselves, we transform our self-esteem. We become our own cheerleaders.

Be consciously aware of any self-talk that tells you you're not good enough or makes you question your abilities or strengths. Create a habit of continual positive self-talk. This will boost your confidence, accelerate the completion of any task, and help you achieve larger goals.

5. STOP THINKING IN BLACK AND WHITE AND ACCEPT THE GRAY AREAS OF LIFE

Cultivating a new, flexible mindset is a daily process. Yes, daily. There will be times when we'll want to revert to our old ways of thinking. I know that when I'm going through pain with my ulcerative colitis, the last thing I want to do is be positive and upbeat. I can get stuck in all-or-nothing thinking, reverting to thinking in absolutes, like I will never ever heal my ulcerative colitis and get out of the pain I'm feeling. When we think like this it's hard to see any light at the end of the tunnel.

How about you? Does that sound familiar? Does stress lead you down the road of either-or? We have to learn to live in the gray, as there are no absolutes in life. Though it may seem uncertain, the gray area is actually freeing. When we find our way to living there, we remove so much pressure from ourselves. Life becomes a lot easier and more filled with possibility.

6. LET GO OF ATTACHMENTS

Having the ability to let go of things and not be fixed on a specific outcome when we set goals is very empowering and freeing. It's not that we shouldn't want to reach our goals. We just need to be careful about locking ourselves into strict time frames or measures of success. That way, when things don't go as planned, we can use our flexibility to pivot and still reach our ultimate goals. Over the years, when I've let go of "what should have happened," a new and better opportunity would present itself to me. But we often can't see those new opportunities if we are stuck thinking that something else is or was supposed to happen a particular way.

7. BE OPEN TO MAKING MISTAKES AND BEING WRONG

None of us ever wants to be wrong or feel like we're wrong. Most of us have been schooled through our whole lives to believe that to be successful in life, we have to be right all the time, and we can't and shouldn't make mistakes. This kind of thinking is completely bogus; if you're still under its spell, it's time to change now!

Sadly, most public school systems have been reinforcing this thinking for far too long, stunting our growth and harming our creativity—it's very hard to take a risk if you're constantly afraid of being wrong or failing.

When we focus constantly on being right, we shut people out. We don't allow ourselves to be coached, trained, or mentored—and so we're not able to grow. Life is about making mistakes, failing forward, and having fun. And remember: while you must make mistakes in life if you want to improve, you yourself are never a mistake.

8. ALLOW OTHERS TO CRITIQUE YOU

We all have blind spots. Thinking you know everything and not being open to constructive criticism can be very harmful. I know this from my own personal experience. There were times when I was younger that I thought I knew everything. I was arrogant and a know-it-all. I had good people around me and should have listened to them, but I didn't, and I paid the price in the end.

Now, not all people have the right advice, though. The trick is to be open to the opinions of others but not married to their takeaways. I like to listen to people and gather as much information as possible, then sit alone and do my own research. When I do this, it allows me to filter through what can help me achieve my goals. Stay open in life and pursue the position of being a student, not a master. And keep in mind that even the greatest "masters" are driven by a constant desire to learn and know more.

9. REFLECT AND TAKE PERSONAL INVENTORY

Personal inventory was something I started taking early on in my recovery journey. It wasn't that I wanted to do it; I *had* to do it to clear my mind. I honestly thought it was a bit stupid and a joke until I found it was actually very therapeutic. Journaling allows me time alone to sit with myself and process my life. Each morning after I wake up, I spend thirty minutes getting my thoughts on paper. Some days, I start off completely angry and frustrated; other days, I feel happy and optimistic. I never know how I will feel when I start writing, and that's the whole point of the process. It helps me reflect on my life, set goals for the future, and deal with my negative thinking. Taking personal inventory through activities like journaling is very important if we want to remain flexible and open to others.

If we don't get our thoughts out on paper, we can sit in petty resentments, anger, jealousy, and other disempowering emotions that are both a waste of time and toxic.

As you practice developing a flexible mindset, it will be helpful to stop and regularly reflect on your progress and the process by which you are changing. In what ways do you see improvements in your approach to learning and evolving?

In what areas can you improve your thinking to make it more flexible? Consider keeping a journal and writing in it each day for at least three months to help you reflect upon and improve your flexible-mindset journey. I've been journaling daily for more than five years now.

10. FOCUS ON WHAT YOU WANT—NOT WHAT YOU DON'T WANT

It's imperative to understand that the way we choose to think, feel, and act is our responsibility. At the same time, however, we also have to be mindful that the seeds of our bad habits may have been planted by the people we spent time with in our early years. We can't change our past or our mistakes, but if we have accountability and take responsibility for who we are in the present moment, we can create the future we want by taking charge of our minds and mindset.

It's been said what we focus on will expand, so it's important that we don't focus on the negative and what we don't want. So here's a question to ask yourself right now: Is your glass half full or half empty? If we see the upside in life and appreciate things for what they are, focusing on what we *do* have, life becomes a lot more joyous.

We do not all enter this world with the same experiences or opportunities. But it is never too late to focus on what you need in this life. Let's say there are two men looking out from a prison cell. One might see the mud on the ground and despair; the other might see the stars in the sky and be filled with wonder. A simple shift in focus can make a huge difference in what we attract in our lives.

Chapter 4

THE IMPORTANCE OF A POSITIVE OUTLOOK

"You should never view your challenges as a disadvantage. Instead, it's important for you to understand that your experience facing and overcoming adversity is actually one of your biggest advantages."
Michelle Obama

Negative thoughts can make us sick and destroy our immune systems. In times of trouble, we need to understand how to reprogram our minds for positivity. We are often not responsible for what has happened to us, but we are always responsible for what we do in the present moment.

The key in life is to learn to reprogram our brains so we can feed ourselves a DOSE of positivity all the time. DOSE stands for dopamine, oxytocin, serotonin, and endorphins. These brain chemicals are our "happy chemicals"; in short, when they are released in our brains, we feel good. Now, we have to be mindful not to make disempowering choices as a shortcut to igniting them. Trust me on this: taking shortcuts isn't worth it in the end.

We'll look more closely at these four chemicals later in the chapter, but know for now that simple things like going for a walk or run in nature, meditating, listening to upbeat happy music, eating healthy foods, and even talking to ourselves in a positive way are all ways that we can all trigger our happy, feel-good chemicals, giving ourselves a DOSE without resorting to taking painkillers, drinking, playing excessive amounts of video games, or eating unhealthy junk foods. By simply adjusting our behavior and getting in the habit of doing easy activities like these, we have a better chance of feeling good and staying on track in whatever endeavors we are pursuing in life.

Consider this: the time it takes to have a negative thought is the same as it takes to have a positive one. So why not make the better, more profitable choice? Disempowering thoughts lead to disempowering emotions. The ripple effect of these emotions keeps us in fight, flight, or freeze mode and can make us physically ill. Review the STOP and STAMP methods explained in the previous chapter. They will help you make the switch from negative thoughts or actions to positive ones, which then lead us to empowering emotions.

Furthermore, negativity thoughts cut us off from our intuition. It's almost impossible to find and hear your Source when negative thoughts and feelings have you disconnected from yourself. The emotions listed on the left side of the below chart keep us disconnected, while the thoughts on the right connect us directly to our Source. If we want to be happy and live our full potential every day, we have to be aware of when we aren't connecting to our Source energy—the invisible, infinite energy we can all access and tap into when we choose. It's not something we can see with our eyes, but we can feel it when we take the time to listen to our intuition.

Negative Emotions	Versus	Positive Emotions
1. Fear		1. Gratitude
2. Shame		2. Love
3. Guilt		3. Joy
4. Jealousy		4. Inspiration
5. Envy		5. Peace

6. Worry	6. Trust
7. Insecurity	7. Empowerment
8. Judgment	8. Appreciation
9. Sadness	9. Empathy
10. Depression	10. Optimism
11. Lust	11. Compassion
12. Doubt	12. Kindness

OVERCOMING OUR PROGRAMMING

Our parents, the environment we grew up in, the food we ate, the places we visited, the TV shows we watched, and the people we interacted with in our early years all play a major role in our programming. Anything we have been exposed to, particularly in our youth, can and will affect the way we think and what we believe in. This in turn affects not only the choices we make on a moment-to-moment basis but also how we view the world around us and the people in it.

Once I started to understand how my brain worked, how it was programmed, and the effects my upbringing had on me, my life was forever changed. I began to see why I had made the disempowering choices I had over the years. I really took the time to take in, study, and process this information to make sure I didn't repeat the same cycles with my son, Orlando. It has taken me many years and a lot of work to reprogram my brain, but reprogramming really is possible.

It can be very hard for anyone who grew up in a toxic, abusive, dysfunctional environment to change the way they respond to triggers and make choices. We have to remember first and foremost that we can't change our past. Then we have to make conscious efforts towards understanding and reprogramming ourselves. People I've coached over the years who've struggled with addiction, trauma, relationship issues, or the loss of a loved one have benefited from the below information. And so will you, if you put it to good use. Our early years are crucial in our development and are shaped by various brainwave cycles (more on those following). A lot of super learners, like Mozart, were coached very early on in their crafts, giving them an edge over the competition. Our subconscious mind is 95 percent of our programming—yes, 95 percent—which means our conscious mind only controls a tiny 5 percent. During these earliest years, we take on beliefs about ourselves and life, many of which will remain in our subconscious mind throughout the rest of our lives. And they will show up in how we behave, the goals we set for ourselves, what we achieve and don't achieve, and even the process of choosing our friends and significant others.

When we are in the delta brainwave cycle as infants, we don't do a lot of critical thinking, reasoning, or judging what is around us; we just absorb what is being fed to us. Notably, studies show that any traumatic events, stress, or agitation a mother experiences during pregnancy can be felt by the baby and then carried by that baby after they are born. As adults, we can reenter this cycle when we are in deep sleep.

Children enter the theta brainwave cycle between the ages of two and six. In this cycle, the brain is still very much under development, and no real critical or rational thinking is going on. Children at this age will take whatever we tell them as the truth, whether they like it or not. Given how much children will absorb at this stage, the theta brainwave cycle is also known as a super-learning phase of a child's development. My son, Orlando, who is four years old, is hugely affected by how I act around him. He is constantly mimicking me and trying to do what I do. It's important we take the responsibility to model good behavior to our kids at this age.

Between the ages of five and eight, children go into the alpha brainwave cycle. This is a very important stage in any child's brain development, as children in this cycle begin to develop analytical skills. A child's imagination still runs wild in this stage, but children in this age range can start to make decisions for themselves. In this cycle, children also start to use both the right and left hemispheres of their brains. Adults can reenter this cycle through meditation. The alpha cycle can be particularly helpful when we are trying to get into a state of flow and creativity.

The beta brainwave cycle starts for us when we're around eight to twelve and then continues throughout our lives. In it, we have the ability to fully analyze life and are fully conscious. However, that doesn't mean we are fully aware and conscious of all the choices we are making.

Take a look at what negative beliefs you may have decided about yourself. As a child, you could have settled on such beliefs for a wide host of reasons, and you've just gotten used to acting on them. But a negative belief is just a *story* you have told yourself. It's not inherently true. It doesn't have to become your reality until you make it so. In 1969, Georgi Lozanov, a Bulgarian scientist, neurologist, psychiatrist, and psychologist, discovered he could help his students retain more information than average students. His technique was called suggestopedia, also known as super learning. I did a little digging and found some interesting studies that were conducted using the suggestopedia technique.

Charles Adamson, a student from Miyagi University, decided to see how the super-learning technique would work when studying a new language. Charles said in a three-hour session he learned the Russian alphabet, some basic sentence structure, and 156 new words. Charles took a Russian test at the end of the class and scored 98 percent. When I read this study, I found it very intriguing.

Lozanov had discovered the power of the theta and alpha brainwaves by playing classical music, relaxing the students and boosting their learning.

When I read about these findings, they blew me away. Having ADHD and dyslexia, I had struggled for years to stay focused and retain important information. So I decided to start my own Lozanov experiment and went on a quest to do what I'd read many top CEOs do: read a book per week. I spent sixty minutes each day reading slowly while playing a Mozart concerto in the background. I struggled the first month to get used to the routine, but then things started to flow. I found that the Mozart music indeed relaxed me. I also found it beneficial to read early in the morning, when there were no distractions. I can comfortably finish a new book every week now and retain most of its information. I still play light classical music whenever I need to read, sit down to write, or focus on a task for long periods of time.

This got me thinking—if I got into a theta brainwave more often, I could reprogram my mind to do almost anything. As I've said, what we focus on expands. I figured I should be able to hack my mind, reprogram the negative programming, and install new, positive programming.

Knowing the ripple effects one negative thought could have, I knew I needed to go deep. And that's what I did. I started doing two meditations a day. The first meditation at 3:30 AM was to get a jump start on my mind. Then I did a second meditation in the afternoon using a theta-brainwave music program. I went on a strict mental diet of only positive information to make sure I weeded the negative stuff correctly.

Did it work? Well, let's see:

- I ran thirty half-marathons in thirty days with a hernia, and not long after stomach surgery.
- I had been told to have my colon removed, as I would never heal naturally. But I did.
- I read a self-help book every week.
- I did more than two hundred speaking gigs in twelve months and successfully fought off some crazy lawsuits—all the while staying focused and happy.
- I'm never sick or tired, and I get up every day between 3:30 and 4:30 AM to meditate and work out.
- I never worry about the future. I know I can create whatever I want or need. I have moved on from the past, not focusing on *why* something happened but instead on how I can learn and grow from it.
- I stay connected to my Source. It guides me day in and day out so I can be of service to others as a coach or mentor to help them find their purpose in life.

THE POWER OF POSITIVE MENTAL REHEARSAL

In 2014, Dr. Judd Biasiotto tested students in a University of Chicago study. They were broken into three groups, then taken to the gym and asked to shoot basketball free throws. An average was taken from all three groups. Then they were told that they would be given special training in order to become better at making free throws.[1]

The first group returned to the gym every day for an hour to practice shooting free throws. Each day, they took their shots and kept a tally of how many they made or missed.

The second group was told to do absolutely nothing (and, specifically, to not practice and not think about free throws at all). They just waited around until the study concluded, and then they were called back in and retested. In other words, this was the control group to ensure the scientific method was working. (If I'd been in the study back during my school days, you can bet your ass I'd have wanted to be in this group—because I hated taking tests, even physical ones.)

The third group was told to come into the gym and visualize through their five senses what it would feel like to shoot free throws. All they had to do was lay on the gym floor, close their eyes, and imagine how making their shots would feel, sound, and look.

After four weeks, the three groups returned to the gym to retest. The group that had practiced shooting every day improved by 24 percent. The group that did nothing showed no improvement whatsoever—go figure. But the group that had completed the visualization exercise improved 23 percent—almost the same improvement as that of the group that had actually practiced.

Personally, I find this study fascinating. I have always made it a point to think greater than my environment, and I believe my success is the result of being consistent, persistent, and focused on what I wanted to manifest in my life.

Highly successful athletes and musicians alike have discovered that mentally rehearsing an event over and over again improves performance. A piano player who mentally rehearses a musical piece will be better prepared to practice it well.

Arnold Schwarzenegger is famous for mentally rehearsing before competitions. He believes his visualizations gave him an edge over his competitors. Even as a young boy, Schwarzenegger's mental fortitude helped him reach his goals; he dreamed at a young age of coming to America to be a bodybuilder and eventually a movie star, just like his idol, Reg Park.

I discovered Donald Hebb while scrolling through the internet one morning, and his theory really got me thinking about the importance of visualization and mental rehearsal. Donald Hebb was a Canadian psychologist whose work and studies were primarily focused on how brain neurons contribute to processes like learning and memory.[2] He studied how people learn, how they prepare themselves mentally for optimal performance, and how they visualize their success. According to Hebb's Law, "When an axon of cell A is near enough to excite cell B and repeatedly or persistently takes part in firing it, some growth process or metabolic change takes place in one or both cells such that A's efficiency, as one of the cells firing B, is increased."[3] This is often paraphrased as "Neurons that fire together wire together." In other words: practice makes perfect.

When I read this, I was very intrigued. Was it true? Could I use Hebb's Law to achieve my goals more quickly if I mentally rehearsed being the person I wanted to be, then acted as if I was that person, regardless of how I felt?

Remember: successful people do the work no matter how they feel. Unsuccessful people only do the work when they feel good or right. Can you afford to take the risk of waiting to feel just right before acting?

GETTING A DOSE AND THE IMPORTANCE OF REPROGRAMMING OUR MINDS

When we're seeking to reprogram our minds for positivity, it's helpful to understand how brain chemicals work. Later in this book, I will go into more detail about the ways to naturally produce them. The short of it is that we are all looking to gain pleasure and avoid pain. As a reminder, we all have four "happy chemicals" in our brain:

D – Dopamine
O – Oxytocin
S – Serotonin
E – Endorphins

I like to say, "We are always looking for our DOSE in life." The trick is to find natural ways to get happy. After I ran thirty half-marathons in thirty days, a guy said to me, "You must love the runner's high you get. It's like doing drugs, right?"

Ah, no—not at all. As someone who's done a fair share of drugs, I can say with confidence that it's nothing like a runner's high.

The way you feel on drugs is what I call an artificial high. That's because they are so disempowering and destructive, and they disconnect us from our Source. The short-term high of drugs gives us the *illusion* that we have the world in the palm of our hands—when, in fact, it is really slipping through our fingers like beach sand.

Now more than ever, we need to get our natural DOSE in empowering ways—not disempowering, destructive, and soul-crushing ones.

HOW DO OUR HAPPY CHEMICALS WORK?

When I went into my postsurgical recovery, I knew I had to understand how my brain worked if I was going to stay sober and avoid becoming hooked on pain pills.

I have never been attracted to pain medication. But back then, sitting in the house, not being able to exercise, and in chronic pain with infections that could kill me—well, anything was possible. As crazy as it sounds, I could have easily used cocaine to mask my pain; but by that point, I knew better.

I love uppers, so I knew I had to look for *natural* ways to dose, or I would slip-slide back to my old destructive ways. Nonaddicts won't understand this, but under stress, the rest of us automatically look to mood alter.

And trust me on this: no matter what people post on social media or say, we all have our own share of disempowering behaviors that can disconnect us from our Source and the truth.

This is the list of drugs I have used over the years: cocaine, heroin, marijuana, prednisone, Norco, OxyContin, and meth. It covers pretty much everything except fentanyl, also known as China Girl and Murder 8. Thank God I didn't use fentanyl—it's become a horrible, soul-snatching drug that hooks you in and eventually kills you (no exaggeration!).

All of the substances I listed can get you high, but each one comes with life-destroying side effects. They all promise so much in the short term but ruin us in the long run. I'm very open about my previous drug use to show people what can be achieved once you understand how we are motivated to seek that high feeling.

As human beings, we are always searching for things that make us happy and that we feel are good for our survival as a species. We feel happy when our "happy" brain chemicals are stimulated and turned on. These chemicals are triggered by different stimuli, so each one creates a different set of feelings.

Let's take a look at how each one works.

D – When dopamine is released in sufficient amounts, it creates feelings of pleasure and reward, which then motivates us to repeat the behavior that produced it in the first place. The "I got it!" feeling, the feeling of getting what you seek—that's dopamine in action. Dopamine drives us to seek rewards, and it's involved in motivation, memory, attention, and the regulation of body movements. Low dopamine levels are linked to reduced motivation and decreased enthusiasm for things that would excite most people. There are some things we can do to *naturally* increase dopamine levels, like going for a run or hike or doing a yoga session or a quiet mindfulness meditation.

O – Oxytocin has gotten the nickname "the love hormone," as studies have shown it is released in the brain when people are intimate with one other. Whether we are cuddling, kissing, having sex, bonding, interacting socially, or playing with their pets, this feel-good hormone is released in our brains. Oxytocin helps us bond, and gives us the comfort of social alliance. It also motivates us to trust others, and to find safety in companionship or camaraderie.

S – Serotonin is a hormone produced by the brain and other parts of the body. What most people don't know is that most of the serotonin in our body is produced in our gastrointestinal tract. Serotonin is credited with helping to produce healthy sleeping patterns and with boosting one's mood. The chemical is commonly linked to feeling good and living longer. Serotonin gives us the feeling of status when we are respected by others. It gives us the security of social importance. It motivates us to seek respect.

E – Endorphins are generated by the body naturally to help us mask pain. When we experience pain, the body produces endorphins as a natural pain killer. I know this from personal experience. When I was running the thirty half-marathons, my body was always sore and stiff, so I felt horrible when I started every race. But without fail, at around the six-mile mark, the pain always went away. All runners know this sensation very well. You may have heard of it as the "runner's high" or as catching a second wind. Once we experience a certain level of pain and discomfort, the brain knows to naturally switch on our endorphins to helps us. If we train ourselves to push through the pain we feel, we can usually get a second wind—and then there's no stopping us.

GETTING YOUR DOSE OF POSITIVITY

Today I understand the importance of managing my mental state because it affects my behavior. As I said before, we are all motivated to avoid pain and gain pleasure. So how do I avoid being tempted by a deadly, disempowering drug like cocaine and not chase that quick hit of dopamine? The answer: by using STOP and STAMP. These techniques are effective ways to slow yourself down so you can redirect yourself to make better choices.

Becoming self-aware of our choices is the key to our success. As humans, we make over 220 decisions a day just regarding food choices.[4] Yes, 220 . . . unbelievable, right? And some of these choices are completely subconscious. Without self-awareness, the brain defaults to the path of least resistance: habits. Habits control not only what we eat, but also almost every other aspect of our lives.

Use the STOP and STAMP techniques to become self-aware. This is key to making good choices and forming empowering habits. Self-awareness helps us recognize temptation, identify behaviors, predict the negative consequences of our behaviors, and make better choices for the long term.

If they put their mind to it, a smoker can recognize that their smoking habit will result in future diseases. And if they can learn to identify the very first signs of the nicotine calling their name, they become better equipped to reject the temptation. Without self-awareness, breaking bad, disempowering habits is futile.

Now that we have a basic understanding of our happy chemicals, let's look at several ways we can naturally get that DOSE we need, ensuring empowering choices and a positive mindset.

EATING TO GET A DOSE

Certain foods are known to boost dopamine and serotonin. Dopamine production is stimulated by the amino acids tyrosine and phenylalanine, which are prevalent in protein-rich foods.[5] Intake of these amino acids, either via foods or supplements, can boost dopamine levels.

The following are some foods containing tyrosine that I personally use today for a natural boost:

- Almonds
- Avocados
- Bananas
- Beef
- Chicken
- Chocolate
- Eggs
- Green Tea
- Milk
- Watermelon
- Yogurt

While you can't pump your brain with dopamine (at least not until some future time when brain-injection home kits are available), there are also supplements that encourage the brain to produce more of it.[6] Here are some that I personally use daily. Notice: *always* consult with your nutritionist or doctor before and while using any of these supplements.

- **Curcumin:** The active ingredient in a popular curry spice, turmeric.
- **Ginkgo Biloba:** A plant that's also a popular "wonder drug." Though it's not scientifically proven, it might help increase dopamine levels by allowing it to stay active in your brain longer.
- **L-theanine:** Increases neurotransmitter production in your brain, including that of dopamine. Green tea has lots of this. Sometimes I take theanine as a supplement instead.
- **N-Acetyl L-Tyrosine:** A production-ready version of tyrosine that makes it easier for the brain to produce dopamine.

EXERCISING TO GET A DOSE

A two-month study in 2006 by psychologist Megan Oaten and biologist Ken Cheng demonstrated the positive effects of exercise. None of the study's participants were regular exercisers. By the end of the study, those exercising at the gym about three times per week showed enhanced self-control, attention span, and an ability to ignore distractions.

But wait—there's more! Throughout the study, participants also reduced their consumption of alcohol, caffeine, cigarettes, and junk food, and they spent less time watching television. They ate healthier food, studied more, procrastinated less, and saved more money. None of this behavior was suggested by the researchers; it all happened spontaneously as a side effect of exercise. Incredibly, participants generally had more willpower and self-discipline as a result of the study—not just in gym attendance, but in all areas of their lives.

A mere twenty minutes (yes, that's all it takes) of exercise can reduce cravings for junk food and cigarettes. Exercise can also serve as an antidepressant. Some people I know who've tried both say exercise is as effective as the Prozac they are taking.

Exercising regularly not only builds our muscles; it also builds our brains. Exercise can increase the volume of both the gray matter (which receives and regulates information) and white matter (which transmits signals other regions of the brain and body) of our brains.[7]

So how much exercise do you need to see these benefits?

As much or as little as you're willing to do. Too many people avoid exercise because they think they need to go to a gym and work up a heavy sweat for at least an hour or two. But even a daily twenty-minute walk around the block can be beneficial.

If an activity raises your heart rate, it's exercise. This includes walking, dancing, gardening, yoga, sports, swimming, playing with kids or pets, and even window shopping (if you don't stop and stare for too long). Any kind of physical activity is good. The more fun it is, the more likely you'll do it regularly. Think about exercise as a way to restore your energy and revitalize yourself.

PROTECTING YOUR DOSE AND YOURSELF

Now, I need to caution you: dopamine triggers can include the sight of tempting food, the smell of brewing coffee, a 50-percent-off sign in a store window or online, or late-night TV infomercials that promise to make us feel better or happier. Our reward system is a product of evolution, and it doesn't care about your happiness; it only cares about survival and reproduction. The reward system uses the promise of happiness to keep you pursuing these goals, whether or not reaching them will actually make you happy.

Unfortunately, our reward system evolved at a caveperson time when craving fatty or sweet foods was a good instinct for survival. But in today's world, food is plentiful, and fast food and many other packaged foods are specifically engineered with fat, sugar, and salt to maximize the dopamine response.

Modern technology floods us with opportunities for instant gratification: Facebook, Twitter, email, and text messaging, to name a few. As a result, our brains are continually searching for rewards, like a quick

YouTube video to make us laugh. Dopamine keeps us constantly refreshing our screens, clicking the next link, and checking our phones compulsively. Video games can also manipulate the reward system, keeping players hooked on their favorite games for hours at a time.

Be aware that marketers and corporations know that we are always looking for pleasure and will do anything to avoid causing us pain. Some of them use this knowledge to get us to spend, spend, spend. Here are some examples of common dopamine rigging:

- Big companies that engineer "foods" loaded with a high combination of sugar, salt, and fat.
- Lottery commercials that show blissfully happy people tossing handfuls of money up in the air to encourage the fantasy of winning that multimillion-dollar jackpot.
- Grocery stores that put the most tempting, eye-catching items in high-traffic areas and checkout lanes. Plus, food samples that make shoppers hungry and put them in a reward-seeking mode to increase impulse buying.

Now, here are four ways we are manipulated by advertising without even knowing it:

1. **Variety Marketing**: Our reward system seeks out novelty and variety, which is why some fast-food chains constantly introduce new items on their menus. Even salads can increase other sales. Some people will accompany healthier-looking options with more French fries, rationalizing, *Well, I'm also eating a salad, which is good for me.*
2. **Offer Marketing**: "Buy one, get one free," "50 percent off," and discounts relative to "suggested retail price" are all dopamine triggers.
3. **Scarcity**: "While supplies last!" or "For a limited time only!" or "Act now! Prices may change!" can cause the reward system to go into overdrive; we think, *I might miss out if I don't buy right now!*

4. **Olfactory Marketing**: Smells can trigger desire. Some fast-food restaurants float the tempting smell of French fries or hamburgers in the air. Some ice cream parlors waft the scent of waffle cones to attract passersby. And some supermarkets hand out yummy samples to lure you into spending more time shopping.

We cannot reach our full potential and live a life of positivity unless we take control of our choices. We need to be aware of what triggers us—and why. We need to understand how we think, feel, and act. But more importantly, we need to have a greater and more constant awareness of what drives and motivates us to make the choices we make. We can't leave all of that lurking in our unconscious, ready to trip us up. By committing to doing the work and staying focused on what you want, the information in this chapter can help you make more empowering choices.

I encourage you to eat right. To STOP and take the time to filter the information from your environment rather than making snap judgments. Set aside time every day to meditate and exercise. Staying conscious and being consistent with positive choices will get you on your way to living a life with *purpose*, which I'll discuss in the next chapter.

Chapter 5

YOUR PURPOSE
IN LIFE

"People don't buy what you do; they buy why you do it."
Simon Sinek

So far, we have worked on reframing our perspective in the present moment and shifting toward a flexible mindset to make empowering choices. And we have taken a positive outlook on life, learned the ripple effect from making this happen, and explored natural ways to get a steady DOSE of positivity. This brings us to the next step: living with *purpose* and working with the spiritual laws of the universe to better connect to our Source.

You might be feeling nervous or skeptical about this step. If so, let's change that. In this chapter, I will discuss several spiritual laws and their significance in connecting us with our Source. Understanding these laws will help you negotiate life and can help reveal your true purpose.

THE LAW OF DHARMA OR PURPOSE IN LIFE

As I frequently tell my clients, "There is a big difference between doing something *on purpose* and the higher state of consciousness of doing something *with a purpose*."

But what does that really mean?

Everyone has a purpose in life . . . a unique gift or a special talent that, when shared with others, makes their lives (and your own) much better. When we use the talent given to us by God and bring value to others by being of service, it not only uplifts the people we bring value to—it makes us feel good as well. I think the ultimate goal in life is to find our purpose and then help others find theirs.

Ready for another Mike Diamond acronym? I believe a person with PURPOSE . . .

P – Possesses an

U – Upbeat,

R – Relentless

P – Passion and

O – Outstanding,

S – Sustained

E – Energy

I personally believe that people who have chosen to be truly authentic and connect with their Source have chosen to live a life of purpose. They understand the importance of having empowering core beliefs, values, and rules—or a code to live by. They are then better able to access their unique gifts more and more often.

Furthermore, these beliefs, values, and rules give them power over their decisions. They understand how to manage their day-to-day actions and choose their short- and long-term priorities. They place significant value on being people of high integrity, living with impeccable standards, and earning the trust and respect of others. They walk the talk—no matter what is going on in the world around them.

THE THREE BRICKLAYERS

Many years ago, I read an amazing story about three men working on a cathedral.

A stranger walked by the three men hard at work and decided to ask them what they were doing.

The first man responded by saying, "I'm laying bricks; it's my job."

The stranger then walked over to the second worker and asked the same question. The second man responded by saying: "I'm putting up a wall; it's my career."

The stranger finally approached the third man and asked the same question. His response was completely different, which caught the stranger off guard.

"I'm building a cathedral," he said. "It's my calling."

So the point of the story is simple. The first man thought he had a job. The second man identified with having a career. The third man felt he had a purpose, mission, and calling.

Once I started to understand the importance of real service to the people around me—rather than simply focusing on the work I do—my life and my perspective changed. It's important to see the big picture of *why* we do what we do, and then take joy in the process along the way (and maybe even fall in love with the work that has no end). That's what life is all about. Life isn't just about going for your passion; it's also about finding *purpose* in all that you do.

The universe calls to us all. That's why it's called a "calling." It's up to us to listen to it and follow the path, no matter what other people tell us. Is this easy to do? Absolutely not. It takes courage to follow our intuition. People will doubt us and question us all the time. And that's okay. We have to remember that our calling isn't a conference call. That's right: it's a call only we can hear, and if we listen to it, daily life becomes an incredible ride.

Focusing on what we want to achieve in life keeps us on track. It gives us forward motivation, and like they say, we can't hit a target we don't see. We have to know what we are looking for before we can make the first step, or else we won't have clear direction.

Again and again in my coaching, I encounter people filled with similar doubts as they are stuck or struggling to find their calling. The following eight questions come up all the time.

---

1. Can anyone find a life purpose?
Yes. A life purpose isn't about getting good grades in school or landing a high-paying job. I know plenty of successful doctors and lawyers who are miserable but feel it's too late to change—or are too scared to start over and do the thing that will give them the most happiness. And I know plenty of people with little or no education who have found their calling and are doing work that nourishes their soul.

2. How important is it to have a purpose?
Purpose is the glue that keeps things together when we hit obstacles. It gives us the drive to keep our candle burning bright during the darkest hours of the night, when all seems lost and hopeless.

3. What's the difference between a purpose and a passion?
I don't believe in passion as a motivator because passion can come and go. Look at athletes who are passionate about playing a sport; once their careers are over, they lose themselves and all their money. It's not about the job—it's about the cause.

4. Do you need money to find your purpose?
You don't need to be rich or highly educated to find your purpose. Just listen to your intuition, do the work, and then follow the road less traveled. Or pave your own road.

5. Can I still make money if I have a purpose?
We never need to focus on making money; it's always a bonus. The key is for us to focus on our purpose and cause. When we make this adjustment, the universe takes care of us and the money will always flow our way, because we know how to use our purpose to bring value to others.

6. Do I need to suffer in pain to find my purpose?
Unfortunately, many people do not really wake up to their callings until they face adversity. Many of us only listen to our calling after we hit the wall and the pain is already there. I know for myself that if I hadn't gone through my stomach surgery and had my son, Orlando, seven weeks premature, I wouldn't have reached my full potential. But now I'm able to use the lessons from those major life events to avoid pain. I stay on track with my purpose now more than ever by occasionally reminding myself of the pain I have suffered in the past. But "gain through pain" doesn't have to be the case for everyone. You could have a simple realization one day that you aren't happy with the status quo and that you want to change *before* things become painful. So you don't have to wait for an epic experience to motivate you to discover your true purpose.

7. Are we born with a purpose?
Yes, we are *all* born with a natural instinct for survival and a need to accomplish our particular purpose. But sometimes life gets in the way, we become distracted—often for years at a time—and we lose sight of our life's mission: to align with our authentic self and live up to our full potential.

8. How will I know when I have found my purpose?
You'll know you've found it when you no longer think about what you are doing as a job. When you discover your purpose, you'll be engrossed in your work and will always have the energy to shine through the toughest of circumstances because the cause behind your work will feel immense and worthwhile. You'll never think of quitting because you'll know the underlying reason for why you're doing what you're doing. When you know your "why," the "what," "how," and "with whom" become easy.

WRITE YOUR MANIFESTO

Many years ago, a man I admired asked me, "What or where do you want to be in life?"

Without even thinking, I rattled off, "I want to be an actor and a writer, and I want to move to America."

He said, "That's great. Now write it down on paper and never lose track of your dream."

I remember when I first encountered Apple's "Think different" advertising slogan. I loved it. I found it edgy and empowering. And it really set Apple apart from the rest of the competition. It made you feel cool to be a member of the Apple culture and tribe:

Here's to the crazy ones. The misfits. The rebels. The troublemakers. The round pegs in the square holes. The ones who see things differently. They're not fond of rules. And they have no respect for the status quo. You can quote them, disagree with them, glorify or vilify them. About the only thing you can't do is ignore them. Because they change things. They push the human race forward. And while some may see them as the crazy ones, we see genius. Because the people who are crazy enough to think they can change the world, are the ones who do.

Inspired by such a powerful and successful campaign, I started to research other slogans and manifestos. All great companies have them—some form of a written statement that publicly declares their vision, goals, or values.

Too often we listen to the opinions of others instead of the voice of our true selves that calls us to do the work we need to do to be the person we need to be. We all have inclinations and talents, but sometimes we're too afraid to pursue them because we worry about what others will think. Writing a personal manifesto is a great way to define our purpose, which helps us stay true to it over time.

Here's my manifesto: "My purpose is to inspire people to reach their full potential. Educate people so they can get unstuck and expand their worldview. Motivate people when they feel lost. Live life to my fullest, love unconditionally, and do work that matters to help others find their truth."

Now it's your turn to build yours.

To zero in on your purpose and start crafting your personal manifesto, begin by answering the following questions as honestly as you can:

1. If you had absolutely nothing to lose, what would you do? And why?
2. What would you love to do, and always felt you could do, but are too afraid to attempt?
3. What have you always known you'd be good at but have never pursued due to money-related concerns?
4. Is there something out there that you feel drawn to, even though some people may think you're crazy for wanting it? What is it, and what's stopping you from pursuing it?
5. What would you love to do if you had all the money you needed right now to accomplish or do it?
6. What would you do if you only had one year to live? What is it that you'd regret not trying during that time?
7. Knowing there are no guarantees in life and that we take nothing with us when we die, what's stopping you from living as your true self and being the best version of you that you could be?
8. Who do you admire? And why do you admire this person? What about them inspires you?
9. Is there someone who has the life you want to live? What are they doing that you are not?
10. What's stopping you from making the choices you want to make right now?
11. Do you feel stuck or lost? If so, what areas of your life do you want to change, and why?
12. Do you have values and rules to live by? If so, what are they? Are they empowering? Do they help you strive to be successful at doing what you love?

Next, we need to buckle down and find the values that really matter to us, define who we are, and exemplify who we want to be. By embracing the values on the following list, I became a dynamic leader. I know that when I live by these values, I'm aligned with my authentic self and my Source. Take a look and note which values most speak to you.

Accountability

Good humor

Adventurousness

Gratitude

Authenticity

Hard work

Commitment

Honesty

Courage

Innovation

Creativity

Loyalty

Consistency

Motivation

Dependability

Open-mindedness

Efficiency

Patience

Environmentalism

Perseverance

Fitness

Positivity

Focus

Reliability

Forgiveness

Taking risks

Generosity

I try to revolve around many of these common values—plus some Mike-specific ones that work best for me. You may have others that are not on the list. Make your own list of values, and then make it a point to live by them.

Finally, rules to live by are equally important and should be paired with our values.

Certain people who like to call themselves "free spirits" cringe when I tell them that they need to live their life according to rules. Yes, *some* rules can confine you. But depending on how you use them, some rules can set you free and open you up to possibilities you never would've had without them. For example, consider these five rules for life:

1. Be yourself on your own terms. Life is too short to live what someone else's dream is for you.
2. Listen to your intuition. It is your guiding light and your guardian angel rolled into one.
3. Look for signs in the universe. They are the language your Source uses to communicate with you.
4. Don't fret over the money. If the *cause* is right, the *effect* will be the money.
5. Always have fun in all you do and be sure to fall in love with the process.

So tell me, you so-called "free spirits"—what's so bad about *those* rules?

Years ago, when I owned Snitch, I heavily valued fun. I was being of service by bringing hugely popular bands to the smallest stage in the world. But my rules for fun back then were: drink a lot, snort a lot of cocaine, and party until 4 AM.

Now my rules for fun are: get up at 4 AM to meditate, do my job to the best of my ability, read daily, run with my son, and keep clients on track for their ultimate success.

Same value of fun—but a different set of rules. Make sure you live by empowering values and rules that take you to a higher standard.

STEPS TO WRITING YOUR MANIFESTO

1. Answer the questions beginning on page 100 to narrow down your true purpose.
2. Review the list of values beginning on page 102 and write a list of the values most important to you, including ones that may not be on my list. Having values and rules to hold you to a higher standard is crucial to delivering on your purpose here in life and reaching your potential. Don't rush this process. And don't write down values that simply sound good. I have worked with many

companies that boast incredible values but never walk the talk. This is an important process for growth and improvement.

3. Define the rules for each of your values. In other words, clarify the expectations for each of your values.

One day, I was in a coaching session with a couple who couldn't agree on anything. I asked the gentleman why he thought he and his wife were being adversarial.

He said, "My wife has no respect."

I said, "That's a good value: respect. What's your rule for that value?"

He looked at me in confusion.

I then asked, "Why do you think your wife is disrespectful?"

"She doesn't wash the dishes," he replied.

I needed more of an explanation. "Can you be more specific?"

He replied, "When I come home from work, I cook dinner. So I expect my wife to do the dishes."

"Have you ever told her that's what you want and expect?"

He had a puzzled look on his face. "Why do I need to tell her? She should know she's being disrespectful."

I kindly explained to him that his wife wasn't a mind reader.

I had the two of them take turns listing three or four of their values. Then I asked them to clarify what their rules were for each one—that is, how they actually expected those values to be lived out. In no time, they were both on the same page about what was important to the other and why.

When we are in disagreement with someone, it's usually because our values and associated rules aren't in sync. It's important that we are clear and honest with the rules we attach to our values—that way we can set boundaries and act with integrity.

4. Now it's time for you to write your manifesto! This is where the fun begins. Find a quiet place, sit down, and think about your dream life. Write down all the things you want to achieve and hold nothing back. This is your Wikipedia page. Your biography. It's your life to live out loud.

Note that when writing your manifesto, you can use language that suggests your achievements, goals, and desires have already happened. For example, instead of "I want to be X, Y, Z," say "I am *now* X, Y, Z." Write it down on paper and never, ever doubt it can't be done.

Remember, this is *your* movie. You are the star.

FINDING UNIVERSAL SPIRITUAL LAWS TO LIVE BY

"When you expand your awareness, seemingly random
events will be seen to fit into a larger purpose."
Deepak Chopra

Defining your purpose and creating your manifesto will set you on your path to success. However, you'll *really* succeed in your career or personal life when you make it a point to bring value to others. This becomes much easier to do when you synchronize yourself with those spiritual laws I mentioned earlier.

There are two types of laws in the universe: man-made laws and spiritual laws. You can violate man-made laws—and may or may not pay the price, depending on whether you get caught. But what happens if we violate spiritual laws? What happens when we are not in sync with the universal flow of energy in the world?

When you violate a spiritual law, it's not a question of *if* you'll get caught. It's always *when* you'll get caught, as the universe sees all.

Have you ever been on the same wavelength as someone? Met them and felt immediately like you'd known them for your whole life? Have you ever thought about a friend or significant other and then suddenly received a call from them? Have you ever known what someone close to you was thinking without being told? Better yet, have you ever envisioned something you wanted to happen and then witnessed it actually happen?

This is your Source (or intuition) at work. We are all made of pure energy. That energy makes up our physical bodies as well as our thoughts and emotions. And it is in constant vibration at varying speeds or frequencies. The energy of our bodies, thoughts, and emotions attracts things into our consciousness that are vibrating at the same frequency—like tuning forks that come together to sound a single note.

When I look at the events of my life and how I won a Green Card in a lottery, allowing me to come to America—that was my Source, my connection to the universe, guiding me.

I am going to focus on just what I consider to be the top six spiritual laws. I have become one with these laws, and they keep me connected to my Source. Whenever I'm off track, stuck, or feeling disturbed, I revisit these laws; they allow me to reconnect to the universe and to my authentic self, and they remind me of my purpose.

1. THE LAW OF ATTRACTION

"The law of attraction states that whatever you focus on, think about, read about, and talk about intensely, you're going to attract more of into your life."
Jack Canfield

What we think and feel matter. When we understand how the law of attraction works, we learn that there are no coincidences in life. Day to day in our lives, we attract the things we focus on the most. We always have a choice to change what we think, what we feel, and where we place our energy and focus.

So if life isn't going the way we like, or if we feel like we are attracting things we don't want in our lives, maybe it's time to examine what we are thinking about, feeling, and focusing on the most.

2. THE LAW OF REFLECTION

"The harmony of natural law . . . reveals an intelligence of such
superiority that, compared with it, all the systematic thinking and
acting of human beings is an utterly insignificant reflection."
Albert Einstein

I heard a saying many years ago that really stuck with me: we are as sick as our secrets. This universal law shows no preferential treatment; it is transparent and honest with us all. The people we meet in our lives and the relationships we have (both good and bad) mirror back aspects of ourselves. When we don't like someone, it's generally not the person that we don't like but the part of ourselves that they are reflecting back to us. When someone annoys us with their impatience, we need to evaluate our own level of patience.

3. THE LAW OF ABUNDANCE

"Today expect something good to happen to you no matter what occurred
yesterday. Realize the past no longer holds you captive. It can only continue to
hurt you if you hold on to it. Let the past go. A simply abundant world awaits."
Sarah Ban Breathnach

The law of abundance is pretty straightforward. It states that we live in an abundant universe with a sufficient amount of money, food, education, housing, and resources for everyone to live happy lives. That may not seem like the truth when we look around at the world, but the universe is generous and will always give us what we need if we do the right work and have the right attitude. This also implies that there is no need to hoard. Having a negative attitude and constantly thinking with a scarcity mindset will affect the abundance we attract in our lives.

4. THE LAW OF CLARITY

"People who lack the clarity, courage, or determination to
follow their own dreams will often find ways to discourage
yours. Live your truth and don't *ever* stop!"
Steve Maraboli

For us to use the universal spiritual law of clarity effectively, we must be clear on what we want to attract and what we want to manifest in our lives. If we are confused or lost, or if we lack focus and clarity, it can affect our creativity and prevent us from seeing new opportunities that may present themselves. It's important we take the time to slow down and start with the smallest details. Sometimes simply starting in a direction can lead to huge momentum to complete a task or realize a goal.

5. THE LAW OF CAUSE AND EFFECT

"Karma is the universal law of cause and effect. You reap what you sow.
You get what you earn. You are what you eat. If you give love, you get love.
Revenge returns itself upon the avenger. What goes around comes around."
Mary T. Browne

The law of cause and effect states that all our actions have a corresponding reaction. That's right: there is always a counter-effect to what we think, say, feel, and do. We get back what we give. This law reminds us to be mindful and very careful about what we say and how we treat others.

6. THE LAW OF GRATITUDE

"Gratitude makes sense of our past, brings peace for
today, and creates a vision for tomorrow."
Melody Beattie

This is the spiritual law that I have probably most tapped into daily. Whenever we are grateful, we tap into the energy of our heart chakra: our center of love for ourselves and others. The energy we produce by truly living with gratitude is felt by anyone we come in contact with.

Energy is contagious. We all know what it's like to be around people who have bad energy or are angry, toxic, and ungrateful. When I wake up, as soon as I put my feet on the ground, I take a moment to think of three things to be grateful for. It has been a life-changing practice. By starting my day this way, things almost always fall into place for me—and even if they don't, I'm still grateful and appreciate life on life's terms.

Growing up, I never heard people talk about gratitude or their appreciation for anything. All they talked about was how miserable life was, despite having everything on a superficial level: money, cars, big houses, boats. They never slowed down to enjoy life's moments and never took the time to be grateful for what they had.

Chapter 6

PERSEVERANCE AND PATIENCE

"That which does not kill us makes us stronger."
Friedrich Nietzsche

I like to say, "Successful people do the work no matter how good they feel. Unsuccessful people only do the work when they feel good." What happens if you are only occasionally feeling good?

Success does not show up by chance. You won't find anyone successful who hasn't made sacrifices or persevered through challenges.

The perfect story to demonstrate perseverance is the Chinese bamboo tree.

Every time I mention this plant at a talk, some people think I made it up. But if you don't believe me, Google it—you'll see it's true. It's an excellent metaphor about life and the importance of having patience, faith, and perseverance to keep doing the work no matter how we feel. You have to fall in love with the process to become extraordinary.

To reach and grow to its full potential in life, a plant has to be cared for. Plants, like people, need nurturing, the right food, a positive and healthy environment, plenty of water, and the right of amount of vitamin D from the sun.

When a Chinese bamboo tree is planted, not a lot happens in the first year, just like when we embark on starting a new business or set out to learn a new skill or task to master in life. But we have to stick to the basics if we want to see any progress.

Now, what's interesting is that the bamboo tree shows absolutely no improvements to the eye in the second, third, and fourth year. At that point, most people will probably throw in the towel and stop watering, feeding, and nurturing the tree.

Most people quit when they don't see quick results in the development of a skill. It's the "microwave mentality"—no one wants the master the basics. But here's what is amazing about the bamboo tree. If you have the patience, play the long game, and do all the work, in year five, something incredible happens: the once-dormant bamboo tree sprouts. In just six to eight weeks, it will grow a whopping sixty to ninety feet. Is this a miracle? No, not at all. The bamboo tree, like anything in life, just needs to have the right foundation to grow to its full potential.

The lesson is obvious: Why don't most people have patience and perseverance when planting the seeds for success in their life? Why do they make one phone call and then get angry if they don't close the deal?

Whenever I coach kids, I teach them the importance of staying the course and not giving up at the first roadblock. So many people fold under pressure. Everyone wants a trophy in life, but only a few are willing to do the training. I know all too well that when I try to cut corners, I end up regretting it.

Earlier in the book, I talked about fighting lawsuits. Unfortunately, over the years, I have blindly signed bad contracts and found myself making deals with shady business partners. On my first record deal, the managers took all my money. I was so desperate to ink a deal, I didn't have a lawyer read my contract. Whenever I've tried to make quick buck or gone against my intuition, the deals I made in the process would later come back to haunt me.

For years I got paid a lot of money to host celebrity events and throw big parties. Some of the deals fell into my lap, and I thought I was bullet-proof. Even when a deal didn't look great on paper, I was so impatient that I'd sign anyway and tell myself I could wing it.

In 2017, shortly after the incident where I was rushed to the hospital with a burst appendix, an old friend asked me to get involved in a NYC restaurant deal in which I'd be a consultant. Once I got out of the hospital, I flew to NYC to get started. Things were a disaster from the get-go, but I thought I could grind it out. How wrong I was. I was traveling back and forth from LA to NYC and advising the restaurant partners, but they could never manage the money right. I was owed thousands of dollars by the time Orlando was born.

Like I explained in an earlier chapter, I made the choice not to go back in order to be there for my wife and son. I gave notice and thought, *Well, thank God that headache is over!*

Twelve months later, a well-dressed gentleman knocked on my door, handed me an official-looking envelope, and announced, "You've been served. See you in court."

It turned out someone in the restaurant had signed my name to a document that made me a personal guarantor to a fish company. The restaurant partners had decided not to pay the bill, so I was on the hook for a $45,000 lien against me and/or my personal property.

All the partners played dumb. It was frustrating. I knew the lawsuit wouldn't just disappear. Now, my initial response was *fight*, not flight or freeze. I immediately wanted to do harm. But I knew through my mindfulness practice to do my best to STOP and create a space between the information I received and my response.

I called my longtime friend Matthew, who was a silent partner in the restaurant and not involved in the day-by-day operation. I asked him, "Do you know anything about this?"

He said, "I don't, but I'll try and get to the bottom of it."

Matthew had also been constantly lied to by the other partners and didn't know they were skipping out on some of the bills. Later on, he would get hit with lawsuits as well.

Matthew got back to me and said, "Don't panic. My sister, Suzan, is an attorney. I'll call her and see if she can help you out."

Suzan took on the case, and we battled it out for the next eighteen months. In the end, she worked out a small settlement. I didn't want to pay anything, but to prove my innocence I would have had to hire independent handwriting experts, which would cost a good deal of money. I knew Suzan had worked out the best deal she could for me. Suzan advised me, "Take it and move on."

I took her advice with the consolation, *Well, that's over!* Or so I thought.

Two months later, I was served with another lawsuit—someone had signed my name for yet another guarantee. A partner was applying for an equipment loan for the business, and they needed someone who had solid credit. Apparently, I was the only one, even though I was only a consultant, not an owner.

When I first signed on to consult, I'd asked if there were any guarantees involved. I was assured there were none. It turned out this particular partner hadn't read the contract correctly. I now know this to be true, since we are settling that lawsuit now, and he has signed forms to acknowledge I never agreed to be liable for any loans, in case of default. It still wasn't easy trying to prove my innocence, and once again I had to hire an attorney to represent me and explain the whole situation to the judge. At the time of this writing, I'm still dealing with the suit, as COVID-19 has caused a delay in all of the courts.

I was able to weather the storms of adversity with calm and aplomb, thanks to the same techniques for patience and perseverance that I talk about onstage and teach my one-on-one clients.

These techniques can help you, too, when you're faced with situations that seem too big to handle.

DON'T TAKE THINGS PERSONALLY

You can be objective by taking yourself out of the picture. What does this mean? Step outside of the problem and view it as if it's happening to someone else. Because if it were, you'd be able to calmly assess the best moves to make and advise that person accordingly. Only, in reality, that person is you.

DON'T SIT IN THE MISTAKE THAT WAS MADE

Do not sit around feeling sorry for yourself. The sooner you start taking action, the sooner the problem is resolved. Action is always the key to creating forward momentum. Sometimes we have trouble just getting off the mark, and that's okay. We just have to commit to diving in and going, no matter how we feel. And when you make a mistake, pivot quickly and get going again. I learned years ago to "enjoy the mess." Remember: a task is hard at the start, messy in the middle, but magical when we look back at what we've created. We never see the mess on the painter's floor at the exhibition—only the finished product. Be willing to make a mess and to love it.

ACCEPT FULL RESPONSIBILITY

Do not point fingers and try to pass blame to someone else. If you put the onus on another person, you've handcuffed yourself—because now you must wait for *them* to decide to solve *your* problem. When you accept full responsibility, that puts *you* in the driver's seat. And this means you have at least some control over the outcome. What's done is done, though, and focusing on what we can't change doesn't change anything. I choose to think of ways to problem-solve, not to feel victimized.

LOOK FOR THE BEST SOLUTION

How many times have you heard the saying, "There's more than one way to skin a cat"? It's such an old cliché that we often ignore its meaning. It means there is never only one solution to a problem. And if you're thinking that there is only one that you must find, you are limiting the otherwise limitless possibilities that are available for you.

One of my default habits when I'm faced with a tough decision is to automatically pick up a pen and pad, brainstorm with myself, and jot down as many options as I can think of. I take a short break. Then I come back and review my list, weighing the pros and cons of each one, and cross them out one by one until I'm down to the winner.

DO YOUR DUE DILIGENCE (I.E., RESEARCH)

I also do a lot of research and read up about what I'm dealing with so I don't go in blind.

Even more important than what you know is to know what you don't know—and to be able to admit this to yourself. This will lead you to the information that is out of your range of perception, knowledge, or understanding. And more often than not, it's just a few clicks on the internet away. And then, once you are well-informed, you'll become a force to be reckoned with.

ASK FOR HELP

Lose your pride if it's in the way. Even the "Lone" Ranger didn't go it alone. He had Tonto on his team.

Sometimes, depending on the situation, you might need a few outside opinions. If this is the case, ask friends or family whose judgment you value and trust. It's when you rush into something and act rashly that most mistakes are made.

Whenever I find myself in a jam—or facing a problem or situation where I'm out of my league—I grab my cell phone and call someone who has more experience than me and can help me navigate through the rough seas. With the major lawsuit, it was my friend Matthew's sister, a lawyer, who came to my rescue.

So slow down and take things moment by moment. Usually, the first thing we do when we get served is panic and think we don't have a fight. That is not true. The law gives us a chance to defend ourselves. Whether a lawsuit or an IRS audit, however, our initial response to these things tends to be fear. We fear what we might have taken away from us. For me, it was my two houses. But I knew I was innocent, and I had to take my time and follow my lawyer's advice to prove it.

Had I not cultivated patience, and if I'd tried to broker an immediate settlement all by myself, I have no doubt I wouldn't have gotten the acceptable deal Suzan negotiated for me. Though it took eighteen months to accomplish it, I still came out way ahead in the end.

If we can stay aligned with our purpose, we can always find solutions. Our commitment can fuel our ability to persevere. Just like with growing the Chinese bamboo tree, you must be patient and have faith. If you dig up your little seed every year to see if it's growing, you'll stunt the tree's growth.

If I'd acted out, snapped on the restaurant partners, went on a witch hunt, or not had the patience to listen to my lawyer's advice, I would have blown up the case for sure. Life isn't always fair. We all have to play the cards we are dealt and not take things personally.

THE CURE FOR COMMON PROCRASTINATION

When people lack the drive and motivation to get going or the patience to finish projects they're working on, one thing always pops up: procrastination. It's a dream killer, and it can affect all of us. I see this all the time when I'm coaching people, and it's something I personally have to be mindful to avoid myself.

Whenever I'm coaching someone, I do my best to help them reach their full potential in all areas of life. But sometimes life is hard, and it can feel like a daily grind to stay on top of things. When my clients are stuck, lost, confused, or feeling like they have no real purpose, one of these things always seems to come out of their mouths:

"I sit around too much and can never get started."
"I lack the necessary drive and can't persevere to the end."
"I'm always on edge and have zero patience."

All three of these disempowering statements will not only keep us stuck and prevent follow-through; they will also make us feel miserable.

From time to time, just about everyone suffers from bouts of procrastination. Even the best of us sometimes find it hard to get going. And even when we know what we should or shouldn't be doing, that doesn't necessarily ensure we stay on course.

But I know that when I try to cram things at the last minute, it only gets me frustrated, and my performance ends up being subpar.

Just recently, someone asked me, "How long do you stare at your shoes before you run?"

I looked at him and said, "What are you talking about? Staring at my shoes doesn't make me run ten miles a day."

It turned out he'd watched a YouTube clip of an athlete saying, "Some days, I'll stare at my shoes for forty-five minutes to get myself motivated to run."

"Sorry," I said to him. "I don't have that much time to waste."

I just start running and know the first hour will always suck, no matter what I tell myself. No amount of pre-run shoe staring can cure that. But somewhere in the next hour, my second wind kicks in, and then it's like I'm on cruise control.

Remember, we all want to experience pleasure and avoid pain; that's life. But here are some techniques that will help you crush the procrastination monster whenever it rears its ugly head.

SET REALISTIC GOALS

Clients come to me all the time saying they want to lose weight and get into shape. The first question I ask is, "How much weight do you want to lose—and what is your timeline?"

Their answer is usually unrealistic. For example: "Thirty pounds in sixty days. I have my wedding coming up." Or, "I want to be in shape for my high school reunion next month."

Now, don't get me wrong; you *can* lose thirty pounds in sixty days, but if you want to do it right and not suffer from any pain or have health issues, you need to be realistic. And you need to get started earlier—not wait until you're in the red zone, then try to crush it with the clock running out.

Often the reason we procrastinate is that the goal we set is way too big and daunting for us to handle. It took time to put on the weight, and it'll take even more time to lose it. It's important to make your goals realistic so that you're not immediately put off by the work required to reach them.

Just like paying off a debt, start with small installments and, if possible, increase the payments gradually over time.

I didn't start running ten miles a day right out of the gate. I started with one mile, then three, and upped the miles weekly until I reached my goal of ten.

CREATE A PEACEFUL WORKPLACE

Life is full of distractions. Our phones have notifications going off all the time. Nowadays, many people work at home with their phones always handy, or even work directly from their phones, so it's helpful to silence nonessential apps or put our phone on "Do Not Disturb" when we need to focus our attention on a work project.

Believe it or not, looking at emails is also a common distraction. I have clients who have become addicted to their inboxes. They check for new emails seven or eight times a day. I, on the other hand, look at my emails twice a day: first after I complete my morning routine, and then a second time in the late afternoon after I get sufficient work done. For some of you, I know this sounds hard, but if you limit this one thing—frequent email checking—you won't find yourself under the gun day after day.

And let's not forget the YouTube temptation—looking at those funny or exciting videos when we should be looking at that dull or boring spreadsheet instead—not to mention the temptations of Facebook, Instagram, Snapchat, and so on that take us down the social media rabbit hole. As I've told my clients with procrastination issues countless times, "Do the work first, then reward yourself with the fun."

Our beautiful pets can be a distraction as well if we aren't careful. As much as I love my dog, he can be a maniac for attention. I make sure to walk him *before* I start writing because otherwise he loves to jump on me and play while I work.

In sum, if you create a distraction-free environment, you'll be better equipped to super-focus on the task at hand.

EVEN SMALL DOSES OF MEDITATION CAN IMPROVE OUR FOCUS AND CONCENTRATION

Sometimes I combine meditation with a light workout while alone in my garage to achieve a sharper focus. I don't know exactly how this combination works, but it does work. Other people I know combine meditation and/or yoga with idea generation or problem-solving. These tools take you to the alpha brainwave cycle, which is a highly creative state.

I also remove myself from my family when I read or write. They now understand how precious this alone time is for me and generously give me my space, saving their "twenty questions" for the end of my workday.

When I sit down to work, besides turning off my phone, I also put on a timer to discipline myself. I'll give myself time limits to complete writing tasks so I don't procrastinate. Like many of you, I have a lot to do every day and a limited amount of time to do it. The timer makes sure I keep myself accountable.

KILL THE HARD STUFF FIRST

I'm big on offense—in other words, being proactive. I like to attack the big stuff first . . . then enjoy the easy tasks at the end. When I run, I take the hills first when my energy is high. Then, in the last part of my run, I cruise home. I have found that when you get the most challenging stuff over first, you can enjoy the rest.

The same is true when facing a fear. Rather than let it nag at you all day long, why not attack it head-on and be done with it? It'll be smooth sailing from there on.

WORK SMART AND HARD

When it comes to work, it's quality over quantity. Thirty minutes of focused attention beats ninety minutes of lackluster effort. Taking an occasional break to refresh and eating super-healthy foods can help you stay focused. Stand up, walk around your desk, whatever. It's important to get the blood flowing. Remember to also avoid foods heavy in sugar, as whatever short bursts of energy they give you will be shortly followed by a hard crash that'll wipe you out.

When you try to grind things out with no breaks or refreshments, yes, you may get your tasks done a few minutes earlier. But your mind and body will be so thrashed, you won't be able to enjoy the accomplishment. The key part of "refreshment" is "refresh"—that is, to revitalize yourself.

HAVE FUN

Yes, fun. I know it sounds stupid, but I'm being serious. Life is short. Many people work so hard, they never enjoy themselves. Consequently, life is one long, constant grind for them. It's pointless to slave away for hours just to be burnt out in the end.

I love my life, even though to some it may seem like I'm grinding. I love waking up early, running, weight training, reading, and living a full life. I hang with people who have great senses of humor. There are no curmudgeons allowed in my circle of friends.

Don't take things too seriously. Inject a spirit of fun into the work you do. Be curious and welcoming to the new and different. Do this, and you won't feel overwhelmed.

Whether I'm working with a client with an addiction or coaching an overstressed executive, people can get very emotional when we start to make changes to grow and reach our full potential. There's a tendency to beat ourselves up when we feel we have failed or hit a wall. I take a more fun approach and have my clients do some role-playing. I have them describe how they would imagine their hero tackling a challenge in their life. When I tell my clients to use this approach, they no longer focus on themselves. This takes them outside of their serious self, allowing them to start enjoying the process of self-improvement. If we don't enjoy the process, then life becomes a grind, day in and day out. We have to learn enjoy the ride.

CULTIVATE PATIENCE—WITH YOURSELF AND OTHERS

Perseverance and patience go hand in hand. If you don't have patience, you'll lack the grit to persevere in the task before you. Unfortunately, many people have limited patience. This is largely due to today's fast-paced world of sound bites, hyper-fast internet speed, and super-short attention spans.

Too often we hear demands like "Give it to me, quick!" or "I need that report on my desk by yesterday!"

I'm always seeing people snap at one another out of impatience because they're not getting their needs met *right now*! While perseverance has never been an issue for me, my temper is something I have to work on constantly. Here are some techniques you can use to have more patience, gain more grit to persevere, and achieve your goals without being a pain in the ass—and I mean to yourself as well as to others.

DON'T SEE SETBACKS AS FAILURES

I have a friend who was great at getting started but lacked patience and could never persevere to finish a project. To him, one speed hump to was a permanent roadblock. He came to me for help and asked me how he could take projects to completion. When I had him review his life, he realized that as a child he was never, ever allowed to fail. Any time there was any pressure, his parents came to the rescue to bail him out. Over the years, he just got used to letting things go after he started a project because there were never any consequences for quitting. While he is very talented and charming, he didn't have any grit or staying power. He also had a lot of fear because he had never pushed himself.

Over a period of a few months, I coached him through the end of a few small projects. Whenever he'd hit a wall, I had him use the STAMP technique. Soon, his fear of failure subsided, and he began to meet roadblocks with the confidence to figure out a way over or around them to continue to the finish line.

Whenever things don't go as planned, which for some people is more often than not, what you need to do is to step back, reflect, and then consider another approach. There's nothing wrong with changing plans, even if you have to start over and over again. Be patient and just stay the course.

It's been said that Thomas Edison embraced failure. He saw it as a necessary component of the invention process. It took him something like three thousand tries to perfect the lightbulb. Each time it didn't work, his attitude was, "Now I know another way *not* to make a lightbulb." And as he eliminated each wrong way, he knew he was closing in on success. And as long as he stayed in the game, Edison had no doubt that it was only a matter of time.[8]

Writing a book is hard for me, being dyslexic and having ADHD. It can be overwhelming to receive initial edits and feedback on my drafts. But I simply step back, reflect on how best to address the changes, and am patient with myself as I slowly work through the rewrites.

ENJOY REJECTION

You read that right. I said *enjoy* rejection. Most self-help books will tell you that you must learn how to *accept* rejection. Not me. I encourage you to take rejection to a whole other level.

Many years ago, when I came to America, I knew I was going to hear "no" a hundred times at auditions before I ever got a "yes." You must have the patience to continually hone your skills and perseverance, no matter how many rejections you get. In line with Thomas Edison, I often tell my clients, "Each 'no' is bringing you one step closer to a 'yes.'" Another way this has been said: "Don't quit five minutes before the miracle happens."

Sylvester Stallone was rejected so many times he lost count. He was even told that he wasn't Italian enough to play an extra in *The Godfather*. But after he wrote *Rocky*, Stallone promised himself that no matter how many times he was rejected, he would never sell the motion picture rights to a studio unless it agreed to let him play the lead. His success is another example of how patience and perseverance win the day.

Producers told Arnold Schwarzenegger it was impossible for him to succeed with his horrible accent. And a young Clint Eastwood was informed, "You'll never be an actor. Get out of the business!"

These legends "enjoyed" rejections—because they all knew the huge talent they had brewing inside of them that nobody else saw. Their will to succeed was ten times stronger than everyone else's doubt. And they were all confident that one day they'd prove the naysayers wrong. Hence, three gigantic box-office stars were made.

Finally, as was said by one of the greatest singers of all time, Frank Sinatra, who in his twenties was rejected countless times by club owners, "The best revenge is massive success."

For myself, every time I'm told, "No, you can't," it's like protein to me. A "no" makes me work twice as hard to prove to them—and more importantly, to myself—"Yes, I can!"

Your rejections are a magical part of your hero's journey. Without them, you have no triumph in your story.

FOCUS ON YOUR PURPOSE

Like I said in the chapter on purpose, your "why" is the glue that keeps things together and on track when life throws us curveballs. I work with plenty of celebrities—trust me when I tell you that just because they have money and fame doesn't mean they are happy and have a sense of purpose. When we live knowing our purpose, it's easy to persevere and be patient. Knowing your "why" and keeping it in the forefront of your mind makes the "how" easy.

WORK ON QUELLING YOUR TRIGGERS

Even with all I've learned, I'm still human. And at times I'll lose patience and come off as rude to people if they don't understand me or if they talk down to me. Throughout my childhood, being yelled at constantly and called stupid, useless, dumb, and a loser made me a little aggressive at times. I have to pause and breathe (three or four deep, sustained breaths) and remind myself not to take things personally. If I'm being pressured by someone, I step back and ask myself, "What's aggravating me in this moment?" Anyone can blow their top when things don't go their way. Winners are the ones who maintain their cool in the middle of chaos—like the quarterback who calmly steps into the pocket and throws a touchdown pass while three defensive linemen are barreling down on him.

Rather than give you the age-old instruction to simply count to ten when you get upset, I advise you to try taking ten deep breaths to calm down. I have taught myself to put my fists in my pockets and just walk away from an argument now. It's just not worth the time, the effort, and the repercussions.

MAKE A LIST OF YOUR LIABILITIES

We all have blind spots—things we don't see that others point out about us. My occasional lack of patience is one of my blind spots. We all have them, as we are all human. Furthermore, we aren't all good at the same things. Developing skills takes time, and we all learn and process differently and at different speeds. When you make a list of the things you are not good at, it will help you be realistic about where you need to improve. And it'll inform you when you need to team up with—or get advice from—someone who excels at what you don't, someone whose strength is your weakness.

What's also important to remember is that we don't have to be good at everything. For example, I'm not very good with my hands. I couldn't care less about building things. My dad yelled at me for years because I showed no interest in fixing things around the house. My wife would occasionally get frustrated with me because I'd use the excuse "I'm not good with my hands," to avoid doing basic chores around the house or putting together any kind of furniture.

Fortunately, I have a couple of friends whose favorite words are "Insert piece A into slot A." Now, if I have to build something, I ask for their help. Mind you, I'm not afraid of hard work. I just don't get any joy out of putting together Ikea bookcases and storage cabinets.

When you become aware of your defects, weak areas, or blind spots, you can work on them daily to improve. Or you can hire help if you have no interest in doing that whatsoever.

LEARN HOW TO FORGIVE

I wasn't truly free until I learned to forgive others for what they've done to me. It's one of the hardest things to do, but in the end, it is most rewarding. Holding resentments is a soul killer. Ruminating over things that can't be changed only taints our perception in the present moment. We can never change what has been done to us, but we can choose how we respond.

Many years ago, I watched a lady forgive the killer of her daughter. It blew me away. After she said a prayer for his family, she went on to say, "I can't get my daughter back, and I can't carry this anger with me forever, either."

From that, I have learned to forgive people even though I don't want to. I've had to admit to myself that I'm human and I make mistakes, too. And if it were the other way around, I'd want them to forgive me.

Forgiving others allows you to move on. Carrying a grudge works against you every time. Plus, it slows you down.

Have patience with other people who are trying to learn. On the other hand, if you find yourself working with a person, even a friend, who is prone to making mistakes, and all the forgiveness in the world isn't going to change that, then you need to sever ties.

A friend of mine, David Meltzer, often says, "Be kind to your future self." This requires not only being able to forgive yourself, but also the ability to do it quickly before things start to fester. We can't be kind to others if we can't first be kind to ourselves. Beating yourself up for mistakes or errors in judgment serves no purpose whatsoever. It leads to a victim mentality.

The solution is simple: see yourself as a work in progress. Like creating a painting, you are applying layer upon layer, adding and subtracting, erasing the failures, improving and fine-tuning the masterpiece.

Finally, know that self-improvement takes time, and it is a never-ending process. And be thankful for that—because if there were an end, you'd be bored stiff.

Chapter 7

INFLUENTIAL PEOPLE

American entrepreneur Jim Rohn is famous for a lot of sayings that hold true time and again. This is one of my favorites: "You are the average of the five people you spend the most time with." In other words, you are strongly influenced by the company you keep. But most people are unaware of this.

Like in any great sports team, while some players have more talent than others, it's the flow of everyone working together rather than each individual performance that makes a winning combination. For example, Michael Jordan may be considered the greatest basketball player of all time, but he has always said that he could not have achieved this acclaim without the help of his teammates.

But what happens if you don't have anyone to help you? Are you completely shipwrecked, or up the creek without a paddle? The answer is no. Even in your darkest hours, just one person—even a stranger—can change the course of your life.

For me, as a youngster, that person was my neighbor, Judy. I was going through a rough patch emotionally after I was kicked out of school. I had no real friends, and my family felt publicly shamed and didn't want anything to do with me. But Judy saw something different in me that no one else did. One day, I was sitting on my porch, feeling down and out. Judy saw me, called me over, and gave me a pep talk that changed my life. As simple as it was, the words she said were magical: "Michael, you are before your time. Prove the haters wrong. And trust me, one day you will look back on these days and know it was all worth it." Then she gave me a badly needed hug, a wink, and a smile.

What Judy did was plant a little seed of hope in me. That's it. A seed of hope and belief that would change the course of my life. After that, I was motivated to get out of small-town Perth and prove to the world who I really was.

Today I do my best to plant seeds of hope in people who are feeling hopeless—to put air in their tires and wind in their sails. Mentoring, even if it's on a small-seed level, is how I pay it forward. It's my "Thank you, Judy!"

FIND YOUR PEOPLE . . . ANYWHERE

Whenever I'm stuck, I look for indirect mentors. An indirect mentor is someone you can read about and be inspired by, even though you don't know them personally or have never met them. This is unlike a direct mentor, who you can physically speak to over the phone or meet in person.

It's easy to find indirect mentors. Successful people and their incredible stories are everywhere; by finding them, we can be inspired to live empowering and extraordinary lives ourselves.

When I was a kid growing up in remote Perth, finding a direct mentor wasn't an option. I had to dream big and hope for the best. But then, one by one, I began "meeting" my indirect mentors, who sat on shelves in the library.

The stories of the following people have inspired me over the years. Perhaps they might inspire you, too. These people learned to bend, not break. They became flexible in their mindsets, and they understood the spiritual laws of the universe. And as I learned more and more about each one, they became indirect mentors to me.

VIKTOR FRANKL

I discovered Viktor Frankl a few years a back, and I wish I had heard of him when I was younger. His work has been studied in medical schools and colleges around the world. Frankl was a neurologist and psychiatrist, and he is best known for developing logotherapy.

Frankl was a Holocaust survivor and, in my opinion, one of the greatest human spirits to walk this earth. One might think that just surviving the death camps would be enough in one person's lifetime. But Frankl went so far as to use those experiences to help others.

As a psychiatrist and neurologist, Frankl was quite successful before he was sent to Auschwitz by the Nazis in 1944. I can't imagine what the experience of the concentration camps must have been like. Being starved, beaten, and tortured, not knowing whether you would make it through the day—it would make anyone lose faith and feel helpless. But quite the opposite happened for Frankl. Observing his fellow captives, Frankl noticed that the people who survived the brutal, unforgiving, dehumanizing conditions all had a sense of purpose.

Frankl found his own purpose while in the concentration camps by giving himself forward motivation. He knew his experience would inspire others. Once he was released, he quickly wrote a book called *Man's Search for Meaning*, documenting his experiences in the concentration camps with a psychological lens. It's a book that changed my life after I read it and has changed the lives of many others, too.

In his seminal book, Frankl wrote: "What was really needed was a fundamental change in our attitude toward life. We had to learn ourselves and, furthermore, we had to teach the despairing men, that it did not really matter what we expected from life, but rather what life expected from us. We needed to stop asking about the meaning of life, and instead think of ourselves as those who were being questioned by life—daily and hourly."[9]

Through Frankl's book, I realized how important perspective is in life. As I write this in the middle of a global pandemic, I am even more aware how important it is for all of us to find purpose and not let stress destroy us.

We all need to focus on causes that bring value to others, not just on our primary wants. I know this can be hard, especially when we are going through hard times, but it's crucial to do so if we want to be happy.

HENRY FORD

Unless you have been living under a rock for, well, forever, you probably know who Henry Ford is. Ford was the founder of the internationally famous Ford Motor Company. Ford was a pioneer and a genius who changed the game around how cars were built by coming up with the idea of the assembly line, which was later used by countless other companies and other industries. What many people may not be aware of is that Ford struggled in his early years. He even went bankrupt multiple times before he had success with the Ford Motor Company.

ALBERT EINSTEIN

Albert Einstein didn't speak with fluency until he was six years old and was actually dyslexic. Late speech is so common for kids with dyslexia, in fact, that it's sometimes called "Einstein syndrome."[10] This has always fascinated and inspired me, being someone who has dyslexia.

To this day, Einstein is considered one of the greatest scientists of the twentieth century. We all know him for challenging Newton's principles around gravity and coming up with the theory of relativity. What many people may not know is that Einstein struggled early on as a student. Although he did well in science and math, he had trouble with English and grammar due to his dyslexia. Consequently, he wasn't a great student, and he would often skip class and have to cram for his exams. At sixteen, Einstein failed his entrance exam to the Swiss Federal Institute of Technology.

Einstein was a freethinker and loved to work at his own pace and alone. Like any good autodidact, he created his own rules. He apparently taught himself geometry at twelve years old and by the age of twenty-six received his PhD. He was awarded the Nobel Prize in Physics and published more than two hundred papers in his years as a scientist. Not bad at all for a kid who didn't speak until he was six years old and struggled in school.

BETHANY HAMILTON

At thirteen years old, while surfing with her best friend early one morning at Tunnels Beach in Kauai, competitive surfer Bethany Hamilton's life changed forever. Going about her business as usual and enjoying the early morning waves, Hamilton suddenly came face to face with a menacing fourteen-foot tiger shark, which bit off her left arm. The bite was so severe, she went into hypovolemic shock and lost nearly 60 percent of her blood. A lot of people wrote her off after the accident, but Hamilton was determined to prove the naysayers wrong. A month after the attack, she was back in the water, surfing again.

Hamilton believed—actually, she *knew*—that she could compete again. Knowing she had to work around not having a left arm, Hamilton hit the gym hard, building up her leg and core strength. She also made adjustments to the equipment she was surfing with. She had a slightly longer and wider board made for her that assisted her when she had to paddle out into the crushing surf to catch waves.

Two years after what could have been a tragic incident, Hamilton proved every one of her critics wrong and was the overall winner of the Explorer Women's division at the National Scholastic Surfing Association's National Championships.[11]

STEPHEN KING

With more than sixty novels to his name, Stephen King is one of the most prolific fiction writers of our time. Now, you would think a talented author like King would have had it easy in his career and that things went along smoothly without a hitch, right? That's far from the truth.

King's first novel, *Carrie*, was actually rejected by thirty publishers . . . that's right, thirty of them. This really blew me away, and it inspired me to keep up the good fight and continue writing no matter how many rejections I got.

I remember seeing an interview in which King said he got so many rejection slips early in his writing career that he used to nail them to his wall in a thick stack. The interviewer looked a little confused and asked him what he did if the nail filled up with slips. "Do you give up?" the guy asked. King smiled at the interviewer and with a cheeky grin said, "Absolutely not. I just buy a bigger nail and keep writing."

J. K. ROWLING

In 2004, the author of the Harry Potter series was named by Forbes as the first author to become a billionaire from writing books. But, like King, things didn't start off so glamorously for Rowling. Rowling struggled in her early writing days. Writing while trying to make ends meet as a single mother was no easy feat. Rowling even supposedly had to sleep in her car for a while, she was so broke. But she didn't throw in the towel on her dream.

After six grueling years, Rowling found a little publishing company to buy her book. For $4,000, she sold her first novel and was off to the races. The book won a British Book Award, and Rowling's series went on to sell more than five hundred million copies and become the number-one best-selling book series of all time.

PEOPLE MAKE THE DIFFERENCE
ENGINES vs. ANCHORS

People can either sink us . . . or help us swim. Love us . . . or hate us. Drive us toward success . . . or hold us back. Put air in our tires . . . or slowly leak it out. As I like to say, people can either be Engines or Anchors.

An Engine is someone who gets behind us and drives us forward. They offer support and constructive criticism, and they don't have a hidden agenda.

Look, everyone has some kind of agenda, and there is nothing innately wrong with that—in most cases, anyway. Here's the important question: Is their agenda working for your benefit or toward your downfall? It's essential to know if a person's agenda is having a positive or negative effect on you.

Take a moment and reflect on a few of the people who are closest to you. Do they have a positive or negative effect on your life?

But don't over-judge them—because we have attracted everyone in our lives by our interpretation of the world around us. Remember the law of attraction: like attracts like, whether we like it or not. And sometimes a person's negativity can boomerang and send us in a positive direction if we're able to put it in perspective.

An Anchor, on the other hand, is someone who doesn't want the best for you. Unfortunately, in life you may meet more Anchors than Engines.

For most of my life, I was surrounded by Anchors—or what some people call haters or naysayers. People who have nothing better to do than try and crush your dreams or control you because you spark fear and insecurities in them by how amazing you are.

Make a list of some of the people who have always been there for you, directly or indirectly. As mentioned above, an indirect mentor is someone you look up to who inspires you. They inspire you by their exemplary actions even though you've never met and may never meet them. A direct mentor is someone who actually spends time with you. Both kinds of mentors are influencers who can help us grow.

Next, make a list of the people who you feel are Anchors in your life, and write the reasons why.

Now review the list and ask yourself why you keep these negative Anchors in your life.

Make a list of at least five direct and ten indirect mentors who are already in your life or who you'd like to add.

To gain power over an Anchor, practice the STAMP method I discussed earlier in the book—but this time, do it with a little twist. When you are brooding over or about to react to an Anchor:

S – Stop.

T – Take a breath in order to control your emotions.

A – Adjust your perception. Remind yourself that they are likely jealous of your success. We can't change people, but we can choose how we react to them. Don't take it personally. Remind yourself that it is just one person's opinion. And it reflects who *they* are—not who you are.

M – Make the change now to see their actions or words with a new, positive perspective.

P – Proceed with power and live your potential.

To succeed in all areas of life, we must have the right people around us.

Fortunately, success leaves clues for others, and these days there are countless resources to discover the techniques and tools used by high achievers. I always look to model the behavior of successful people. Great athletes do it all the time, modeling themselves after their own sports heroes. Most business entrepreneurs do this as well.

TOXIC ANCHORS

Like I explained before, neurons that fire together wire together. If you are in an abusive relationship, you will constantly feel unsafe. And when we feel unsafe, what happens? That's right—we go into fight, flight, or freeze mode. Over time, that will break down your immune system, causing ongoing stress to your body. Under attack, our emotions can hijack us.

Back in the day, after years of working in the nightclub business and getting into fights, I was always looking to attack people. No matter how mindful I was, having people scream at me night after night made me want to just snap and throw a punch rather than try to reason with anyone.

But now I've learned to synchronize with anyone I want, and I'm going to show you how to do the same. Remember: you don't need to try and change people to get along with them. To truly understand people, we first have to understand ourselves. Being aware of how we look at the world allows us to comprehend how others see the world in their own particular way. When we become self-aware, we can have compassion and empathy for others.

Everyone has different perspectives of reality based on what we have experienced up to this point in time, whether good or bad. But we don't have to keep suffering through trauma if we are willing to become mindful. Think about it this way: If I told you to watch the worst movie you'd ever seen over and over again, would you do it?

Of course you wouldn't. If I asked for a reason, you'd probably reply, "Why would I replay something over and over again that I don't like?"

Well, think about this. Yesterday is done. What has happened has happened and can't be changed. So why do we keep replaying the same old movies (i.e., the bad experiences in our past) in our heads when they only make us sick, angry, and resentful and prevent us from making empowering choices?

We let naysayers and Anchors rent space in our heads. If your mind is a multimillion-dollar apartment, make sure you have good tenants.

HOW TO SYNCHRONIZE WITH ANYONE AND CREATE A MASTER TEAM

Being able to build rapport or synchronize with others is both empowering and exciting. But if you try to change people or make them do things they don't feel inclined to do, it'll backfire on you. It's far more important to listen to people and then understand why they are making the choices they are making.

Knowing how we personally process information better enables us to understand how others behave and why. Let's take a look at the different ways people can sort out information:

Someone Who Looks at the Big Picture Versus Someone Who Wants Details

A visionary isn't someone who wants a lot of details. A visionary wants the big picture so they can look at the overall purpose and mission. They leave the intricacies of the plan to more detail-oriented people. Understanding both levels of perspective is important to your success. We must have macro goals—a "why," a purpose, a mission. But just as important is creating a plan to reach those goals—knowing how we're going to do it and who we want on our team.

When you listen carefully to how someone talks, you can ascertain how much detail, if any, they go into when explaining or describing an event. Listen for clues in the conversation so you can synchronize with anyone at the level of detail most natural to them.

I, for instance, have big dreams, but I also love to rave on and on about the process of achieving them, which can be annoying to some people. My wife, on the other hand, is all about the big picture. Details bore her to death. For years, I'd get upset that she wasn't paying attention to my stories until I realized she didn't want or need all the minute details to understand my point.

Here's an easy way to see how a person sorts information. Next time you're in a conversation with someone, just ask them a simple question like "What did you do last night?"

A big-picture person will keep it simple. "I got home around 8 PM after work, ate dinner, watched a little sports, then went to bed." Not a lot of information, but you get the picture.

Now, a detailed person will give you way more information: "Last night was a disaster on the road. It took over ninety minutes to get home because there was a horrible accident on the 101 Freeway. Motorcycle versus SUV. I was so beat because my boss has been grinding me lately on deadlines. All I wanted to do was eat some dinner, put on the Lakers game, and relax. But people wouldn't stop tagging me in photos on Facebook, which causes my iPhone to *Ding! Ding! Ding!* So, of course, I have to respond and like each one. And then I got a call from Mom, and she went on and on about . . ."

By now, I'm sure you can see the difference. So if you're dealing with a big-picture thinker, keep it to the vision and mission at hand. Don't overload your story or explanation with nonessential details. On the other hand, if you're dealing with a detailed person, you have to break things down to their liking. Neither is wrong or right. You just want to be able to identify both kinds of people so you can most effectively grow relationships with them.

Steve Jobs was a big-picture thinker. But he needed his highly detailed engineering team and support staff to bring his dreams to fruition.

Until I know which type I'm dealing with, I do my best to keep my conversations somewhere in the middle. By being a good listener, I can easily determine if the other person prefers the big picture or is detail oriented. I then gauge what I say accordingly. I now have several highly productive business relationships as a result of figuring out the type of person I was dealing with first and then adjusting to the preferred communication style.

There is no right or wrong way to do this. It's simply a matter of recognizing how people process information, getting your ego out of the way (the "my way or the highway" attitude), and then putting your ideas in terms *they* best relate to.

Matcher Versus Mismatcher

Matchers are generally easy to get along with. They look for things that they can relate to. Dealing with a Mismatcher, however, tends to be more difficult, as they look for and focus on differences.

Overall, a Matcher is easy to synchronize and get into the flow with. Someone who mismatches, on the other hand, can make you feel uneasy. Mismatchers are pessimistic people, whereas matchers are optimists.

When I'm working on a project and come across a Mismatcher, I have learned to hear them out. Sometimes their critical thinking can be very important, and I'd prefer to err on the side of caution than go all in with no regard to criticism. Just because someone is a Mismatcher or a little pessimistic doesn't mean they are all wrong or a bad person. With important decisions, it's helpful to get several different opinions before moving forward. In the past, I'd always battle with Mismatchers and take their words personally, feeling that they were set out to crush my dreams. But now I feel it's important to take in all the information, sit with it, and then make the best choices available to you. Sometimes a Mismatcher can help you reach a compromise that benefits all.

Sensors Versus Intuitives

A Sensor has a completely different approach than someone who uses their intuition to solve problems. Sensors like data and facts. They are detail oriented and love things they can see, feel, and touch. A Sensor likes concrete tasks and usually prefers things in a linear sequence. Sensors easily follow directions and like to stick to the plan.

Intuitive people prefer the big picture, see all the possibilities, and ultimately follow their gut instincts. An Intuitive likes to read between the lines. They are abstract, creative thinkers. People who follow their intuition can get bored easily and feel bogged down by details and monotonous tasks. They are always looking to do things outside the box and try new ways to solve problems.

Both Sensors and Intuitives have their strengths and weaknesses. Understanding both helps us determine what style best aligns with what we want to achieve.

I generally follow my gut, but I've learned that if I don't have good, detailed Sensor types around me, things can fall apart easily and go off course. I have worked with a few Intuitive visionaries who blew up projects because they were optimistically delusional. I have also worked with overly detailed Sensors who were so painstaking and inflexible that they got stuck when the situation quickly changed and weren't able to go with the flow.

Once I understand the type of person I'm working with, I can correct or adjust in order to achieve a successful outcome.

Black or White Versus Gray

When a person sees only black or white, it's either this or that—there's no in-between solution. They are sometimes referred to as closed-minded. Those who see gray, however, tend to be more open-minded. They see merit in both the black and the white, and they are the ones who come up with a compromise that encompasses aspects of both.

If we have strong values and rules and live by a code that's empowering, seeing things in black or white (or working with someone who does) can be useful, keeping us steady on the track we've created. This perspective only becomes disempowering when it starts to keep us locked in a fixed way of thinking. If we have no choice but to work with someone who has an all-or-nothing, black-or-white fixed mindset, we have to be flexible and find a way not to judge them but to flow with them. Showing a black-or-white person that each of two ideas contains some merit can move a stuck project forward.

WHY VERSUS HOW

Having a "why" is important, but being stuck in asking, *Why is this happening to me?* puts you at a disadvantage and works against you the more you obsess about it. It's okay to look at a situation and ponder why something has occurred if things didn't go our way. But to sit on *Why me?* is unproductive.

Have a "why"—that is, a purpose—understand the "why," and then move to the "how." How can I learn from this situation? How can I grow from this experience? People who stay in *Why me?* mode develop a victim mentality. People who understand the "why" and move on to the "how" become problem solvers.

When someone is stuck ruminating over a long-gone bad experience, do your best to understand them, and then show them a new, positive way of looking at it. If necessary, use an example from your own history where a so-called bad experience led you in a new direction that you would not have otherwise taken and had a profitable outcome.

A recurring theme that comes up in my coaching sessions is the obsession over one's failures. People get stuck in their past setbacks and believe that because something didn't go as planned before, it'll never work out in the future, either. But whether it's a breakup, losing a job, or failing a test, there is always a lesson we can learn.

When I'm dealing with a client who is stuck in this kind of thinking, I work on reframing their perspective. I explain that it's important to learn and grow from the experience so it doesn't repeat itself. Then I show them how to set up a better plan and look at things that may become obstacles in the future.

People often ask me why I'm so open about my prior drug and alcohol abuse and whether I worry about what people may think about it. I'm honest and tell them that my past isn't my present or my future. If we understand our "why" and are willing to accept help, things will always fall into place. I wouldn't be the coach I am today if it weren't for the number of times I have failed in the past.

Years ago, when I was raising money to open a nightclub—my first big venture—a good friend set me up with a potential investor. The two of us sat down, and before I could even get going with my proposal, he held up a hand and asked me, point-blank, "How many businesses of yours have failed?"

I was caught off guard but, rolling with my usual confidence, proudly told him, "I haven't failed at any."

"Well," he replied, "go out and fail a few times, and then come back to me."

I was stunned.

He went on to say, "You don't know how to keep a business going through the hard times if you haven't lost at least one or two. You need to experience the taste of failure before you can succeed."

So I wasn't surprised when that same investor offered to back me on another nightclub project after I'd had a couple flops.

BEST CASE VERSUS WORST CASE

In hard times, being able to look at a situation and understand what the best-case versus worst-case scenarios are can be a true gift. Choosing optimism over pessimism and being the person who looks for opportunities to grow on a day-to-day basis is empowering in a huge way. Focusing on only what could go wrong in the worst-case scenario keeps us stuck in survival mode. We all need a sense of security and to get our needs met, but always thinking about the worst case in order to prepare for it results in a limited mindset. A best-case, glass-half-full look at the world, as opposed to a glass-half-empty one, helps us have gratitude.

I never really understood the power of gratitude until I read about people like Viktor Frankl and Nelson Mandela. Mandela was locked up in prison for twenty-seven years and never held a grudge. Frankl, as I explained earlier, was the king of finding gratitude in even the toughest moments.

It's important to wake up every morning and be grateful for the small things in life. Gratitude has a positive ripple effect on how our day goes. And when I say small things, I truly mean it. You can simply give thanks when you wake up in the morning that you are alive. Every day, I am grateful that I have food to eat, a comfortable bed, a loving wife, and a healthy baby boy.

Whenever I feel that someone has mistreated me, I find things to be grateful for right away—otherwise, my resentment builds quickly and gets out of control.

What we feel within, we push out onto the world. Squeeze a lemon, and you get lemon juice. Give an ungrateful person one million dollars, and they will find something to complain about. Having gratitude connects us with our Source. Gratitude greases the wheel that turns our fortune.

WHY CAN'T WE ALL GET ALONG?

Under stress, different people act differently. Some people are passive. Some are aggressive. Some are assertive. When times are tough, we all react according to how we've been unconsciously conditioned by others or how we consciously conditioned ourselves. Therefore, it's good to STOP and allow others to be themselves rather than judge them. And if they need help, then step up and offer a helping hand.

Do you become passive under pressure? If so, why? Has it served you? If not, how can you change?

Are you aggressive under pressure? If you are, have there been times when you felt that your aggression worked in your best interest? Have there been times when it has caused you harm and ruined relationships?

Some people are active, others reflective, and then there are those who are inactive and become frozen when faced with adversity.

Which are you? Active, jumping straight into a problem? Or inactive, where you freeze up or feel stuck? Or are you reflective, thinking through everything that has happened before proceeding?

Active people are doers and look at the big picture. They are forward thinking and try to push themselves and others to reach their goals. They don't sit in the pain of their problems too long because they know life is short and that an opportunity can fly right by if you don't grab it by the horns.

Reflective people like to sit with information and ask a lot of questions before they take action. And inactive people do nothing at all. Obviously, being inactive isn't the best approach to problem solving. If you frequently find yourself stuck in inactivity, it's important to reach out and ask for help.

We all have different drivers. Some of us sort through people. Others, places. Others, things. Understanding how you generally operate is critical in learning how to match and synchronize with other people.

You can think about it this way: If you were planning a holiday or a vacation, what would be your primary interest? Would you be going to a destination because of the people you might meet there? Or because of the place itself, for its beauty and awe-inspiring landscape? Or would it be because of the things and activities to partake in while there? Or would you go for the location's rich history?

When I go on vacation, I'm most concerned about the people around me. If the people I'm with aren't friendly and warm, I don't really enjoy the place as much.

Now, let's say we are discussing different topics: health, politics, and religion. What catches your attention most—the person delivering the message, or the discussion itself?

Those who pick the former option will "attack" the person to get the answers they seek, whereas those who pick the latter will "attack" the information presented for answers.

One judges the behavior of the person. The other judges the value of the information. I personally look at the person more than the information.

It's important to understand that we are all different and process things differently. Take a moment to ask yourself how your mind sorts information. Does your primary interest focus more on people, places, things, activities, or information?

People also process information differently when making a decision to purchase something. We typically sort the decision out in one of four ways: cost, time, quality, and convenience. Which one are you primarily concerned about when considering a purchase? Pay attention to how you and those around you prioritize these four areas.

If someone wants quality and convenience over cost, it's pointless telling them how much money they are going to save in the future. You'll form an alliance with that person by instead giving them examples showcasing the item's high quality and convenience.

On the other hand, if someone is mostly concerned about cost, there is little point in focusing on quality. To this person, "What's the lowest price I can pay?" is the clincher. So don't try to sell them on the value retention or the prestige of ownership.

What about someone who looks for convenience? Regardless of cost or quality, convenience-focused buyers are only interested in what's easy. For example, if it's food, they want to know how easy it'll be to make. They don't own any recipe books. Their freezer is stuffed to the gills with microwaveable foods. If it's a product, they ask, "Is it easy to use?" This person will gladly pay much more for an already assembled desk than for a cheaper Ikea DIY model of the same quality. They don't read owner's manuals. And if it's a business transaction, don't come to them with a fifty-page contract cluttered with fine print. They love handshake deals. Keep it simple: "You do this. I do that. And we both make out like bandits! Put 'er there." (Picture a glad hand proffered.)

There two types of people when it comes to time. Those who work best with deadlines are called "through-time" people. The converse is people who go with the flow. These individuals are called "in-time" people. Most artists are in-time types and get lost in their projects. I have worked with musicians who can get lost, seemingly forever, when writing a song and have no idea what time or even what day it is.

Conversely, an engineer or builder might prefer a specific plan and structure to work on a project. Or they may have been given a due date they're required to hit, or else it will cost them money. Most through-time people actually prefer a deadline or milestones to hit along a lengthy project. That is what keeps them focused—what keeps their eye on the prize.

When working with either kind of person, it's important to understand how they value their time and how convenient or inconvenient their time is to them.

An in-time person may love the experience of physically going to a shop to buy something. Because who knows? They may serendipitously stumble upon an item they weren't even looking for—but that turns out to be better than the item they were supposed to find.

However, a through-time person will prefer the convenience of, say, Amazon Prime, as they have deadlines to meet and consider it a waste of time to wander around shops all day.

What's convenient for me may not be convenient for you. My wife gets totally lost and absorbed in certain things that I find annoying, and vice versa. For me, window-shopping makes no sense. I walk into a shop knowing what I am going to buy, I buy it, and then I'm done.

Neither way is right or wrong—it's just how people choose to manage their time based on their circumstances. When we recognize and understand how someone values time, we can see what is convenient or inconvenient for them. And, equipped with a better understanding of others, we can more easily get along with them.

Finally, here's a little-known secret: the best thing you can do to get along with most people is to refrain from trying to change them. Let go of trying to convince people who they need to be and why. Your need to control is more about you than them, and most people will recognize that. Instead, strive to truly understand others. Work with their strengths and help them shore up their weaknesses. But only do this if they are open to your suggestions. Do not attempt to force your uninvited opinions on others. It will only serve to further drive a wedge between you and them. Always ask for their permission first, and only if they agree to listen should you voice your opinion about the changes they should make.

If we listen to our Source and know we are all doing our best, then we can let people do what they do, and we can more easily synchronize with the people we feel will and can help us achieve our goals.

There are only twenty-four hours in a day, so it helps to know why we want what we want—and why others want what they want. When you can identify the people who will help you strengthen areas where you are weak, it allows you to achieve the things you want more quickly and efficiently. At the same time, your understanding of what makes people tick—what drives *their* wants and needs—will help you put together a winning team.

Chapter 8

BRING PLACE TO YOU BY MASTERING TIME

Growing up, I heard people say things like this all the time: "I can never seem to catch a break," "I have the worst luck and things never go my way," "I always seem be in the wrong place at the wrong time."

Hearing people say things like that got me thinking about life and what happens to us, good and bad. Are some people luckier than others? Are some people destined for greatness while other people are destined to fail? Do we have a choice, or is our fate determined as soon as we are born? Why is it that some people win fortunes while others are hit with massive disasters and disease? We see some people live into their nineties, people who weren't nice and did harm to others. Meanwhile, innocent children die before they even become teenagers.

Some people think I've been lucky based on the opportunities I've had in my life. Maybe they're right. And maybe they're not. I'm not sure. But what I have found over the years is that there will be both good times and bad times. Nothing is ever set in stone or certain, and the only thing we can control is how we respond to what's happening to us in the present moment, which of course will also affect our future moments.

What if luck is something we can create by actively working to be in the right places at the right times? Roman philosopher Seneca is attributed with saying that "Luck is what happens when preparation meets opportunity." I agree completely. In my life, things always seem to fall into place when I allow my intuition to guide me, and I get out of the way. The universe is the ultimate GPS. If we are specific with what we ask for and listen well, miracles can occur. In the book *The Secret*, author Rhonda Byrne writes about the law of attraction, the idea that if you ask for something, inviting it in, you shall receive it. I like to add a spin to that: ask, believe, listen to your intuition for guidance, then take massive action—and I mean *massive* action—and you shall receive what you are destined to receive.

Back in 2009, when I first moved to Sin City, I was opening a restaurant lounge in the Mandalay Bay Resort and Casino. I was hired as the marketing director for a company called the Opium Group. Every Monday night, I would take my staff out to other nightlife venues on the Las Vegas strip. I had two motivations for doing this. One was to let my staff have some fun. The second reason was to promote the opening of the place we were about to launch. We would always roll twenty to thirty people deep. The other nightlife venues appreciated our support and would roll out the red carpet for us. Little did I know that my charitable approach would actually help me in the future.

One day while I was on my way to meet my staff at the Wynn casino, I was pulled over by a traffic cop for running a red light. To be completely honest, it was an amber light that turned red as I made a left turn from the 15 Freeway north onto Las Vegas Boulevard. I thought nothing of it at the time, but the traffic cop wasn't too happy with me. He asked me for the usuals, license and registration, which I provided to him. But there was one little issue: I didn't have an American driver's license at the time, only an Australian one. The traffic cop immediately got suspicious and started asking me questions, but I stayed cool and remained in my car. The officer went back to his motorcycle, which was parked behind me, and started to write up some tickets. I ended up siting there for close to thirty minutes, my mind racing over what he could be doing. None of it was good. I was pretty sure I might be spending the night in jail for driving on an international driver's license, even though I'd thought it was legal for me to do so.

Then, from out of nowhere, another police car drove by, and the driver called out my name. I had no clue who he was as he pulled up beside my car and jumped out with another officer. Was I going to jail? Had the traffic cop called for backup for some reason?

"You're Mike Diamond, right?" one of the newly arrived officers asked.

"Yeah," I admitted, unsure if I should have. "Look, I know I ran a red light and have an international driver's license. Am I going to jail?"

The officer started laughing, which completely threw me off, but I kind of smiled and gave a little chuckle back. "Look," he said, "you don't know me, but I know you. I date one of your bartenders, and you always comp my drinks when we go out with your group to promote. I always show up late to meet my girlfriend, and you're always too busy for me to introduce myself and say thank you for always comping our drinks and taking great care of us. So here is my thank you. The tickets are gone. Have a great night."

I was in complete shock. "Are you serious? I'm not getting a ticket for running a red light?"

The officer smiled at me and tore the tickets up. "Absolutely not, buddy—or should I say 'mate'?" Then he handed me his business card. "I'm Sheriff Jones, and I'm always on the Strip if you ever need anything."

This is one small example, but the point is that if we are good, kind, generous, and outgoing, then the ripple effect can be huge. We never know the people we might affect when we do the right thing. Over the years, I have found that if I have good intentions and do good deeds, things fall into place for me.

IS TIME YOUR BEST FRIEND OR WORST?

Place is about more than just location; it also relates to how we use the time we have in our arsenal. In fact, one of the most important things to master when figuring out how to use place to your benefit is the skill of time management. Time is one of the most valuable resources that you have. But many of us waste so much of it, going about our day haphazardly or arbitrarily without a game plan.

There is one thing that can never be replaced or stored for later, no amount how smart, funny, or talented we are: time. No matter where we go or what we do, time will keep moving forward. I got a second chance at life after my stomach surgery. Ever since that day, I have had a completely different relationship with time. I understand how precious it is and try not to take it for granted or waste it—because once it's gone, it's gone forever.

Take a look at your needs and wants. Are you wasting time on things that really have no value? Things that give you momentary pleasure in the short run but have no payoff in your future? Take a moment to seriously think about how you make use of your time. Do you waste hours each day doing nothing or doing things that are nonproductive?

Consider this: How much time do you spend on television, binge-watching the latest series? Or watching reality TV? Or other programs that bring you no value? What *are* you watching on TV? Does it bring you any value, or are you just sitting in front on the television, watching mindless programs to distract yourself? Are you getting a return on the time you spend watching TV?

We're all familiar with the financial term ROI (return on investment). I am going to add a letter, then ask you to consider: What is your ROTI (return on time investment)? How much of the time you spend on an average day is going to pay you dividends in the future?

At the end of a given day, look back and reflect upon how you invested your time, then ask yourself: "How many hours did I spend watching pointless television, having fun on social media, or just frittering it away?"

How do you think you will feel at eighty or ninety years old? Will you look back over your life and think, "God, I wasted so much time watching television shows and programs that brought me no value"? Or will you look back over your life and say, "Man, I lived to my fullest, reached my potential, and achieved all my goals"? When people who only have weeks to live are interviewed, a common truth comes to the surface: they all wish they had more time. They regret that they wasted time doing things to please others and didn't spend enough time pursuing their dreams and purpose.

I assure you this: you're only going to regret the things you didn't do.

So, I urge you—don't waste another moment. Make sure you live, love, matter, inspire, motivate, and empower other people along the way.

Think of what you could do with your downtime to increase your personal value. What else do you think you could be doing that could help you learn or grow? For example, you could be reading self-help or how-to information. Learning a new language. Watching something inspirational.

Whenever I'm not working my regular jobs (speaking on Zoom, coaching, or training), I'm busy writing two books. I also do a weekly live show with my good friend David Meltzer called *DOSE from David & Diamond*. I'm also a cohost of the *Recovery Today* magazine podcast with Rob Hannley, which we shoot weekly. And on Fridays, I do a fun motivational video series called *Friday Fire* to help people kick-start their weekends.

This is not meant to shame you or say you should never indulge in some fun on the internet or TV. Rather, be aware and careful that those things do not become daily time-consuming habits.

Shortly after my son, Orlando, was born, I began to manage my time differently. I started to get up at 4 AM and did my morning run while pushing him in a stroller. I also put together a home gym, but I didn't have a lot of equipment to start with, so I improvised. I started using Orlando as my weight vest while doing pull-ups—and let me tell you, it's no joke. I shot and posted some clips that got the attention of a company called LÍLLÉbaby. They loved the videos of Orlando and me working out together and sent me some baby carriers. Spending time with my son in the early mornings has been amazing, and it allows my wife a few extra hours to sleep, which has been a lifesaver in our marriage.

Pushing Orlando in the stroller inspired me to enter my first half-marathon, which I ran while pushing him along the way. We had a blast together. I found a real passion for running again and decided to run for a cause.

A friend's daughter, Layla, had been struggling with an autoimmune disease, and unfortunately, the doctors had hit a wall in her treatment protocol. I decided to run thirty half-marathons in thirty days to raise money for medical research to help the family find alternative treatments.

Now, you may be wondering why I picked thirty half-marathons in thirty days. Well, I did some research on the internet (time well spent) and discovered that the Guinness World Record was twenty-one half-marathons. So, I thought, why not use an attempt at a new world record to bring more awareness to Layla's cause? I completed the thirty half-marathons and broke the world record. We raised enough money to pay for the first part of the medical research. We shot promo videos and were very active on social media, which created some great press for Layla's cause.

TIME TRAVELING

Let's play a little game with time. Let's say your daily commute is sixty minutes to and from work every day, which works out to be two hours total. Now, you do this commute five days a week, which is ten hours every week of commuting. Now, those ten hours per week equals forty hours per month, which in turn is 480 hours of driving in your car per year. Yes, 480 hours spent driving to and from work.

Now, how do you use this time? Are you listening to the same songs you heard the day before? And the day before that? Or are you listening to those radio talk shows where the host rants and raves about his political viewpoint that you already agree with? How could you use this time more wisely?

When I took the job teaching the kids in lockdown, some days I was driving eight hours back and forth. So I decided to turn my car into an information library. I had books on tape playing nonstop. I didn't waste a minute and loved the drives. I associate so much happiness and pleasure with learning in my car.

There were three books I listened to multiple times to ingrain the information. The first was *Start with Why* by Simon Sinek. I tell everyone to read this book. Sinek has a great approach to building a company and becoming an inspiring leader. It's done by finding your "why" before you look at what to do and how to do it. Sinek explains the importance of knowing your "why" and how the best and most successful businesspeople have followed this same approach and achieved great results.

Maximum Achievement by Brian Tracy covers a lot of amazing topics about personal success in a simple way for anyone to understand. I really love the way Tracy gives his audience an honest, straightforward message. He packs this book with loads of information and tools that can be applied to living our full potential in life.

And last but not least, *The Ego is the Enemy* by Ryan Holiday. I'm a big fan of Holiday's books, especially *The Obstacle Is the Way*. Holiday has a great way of breaking down stoicism for anyone to understand and apply to living in the twenty-first century.

If you struggle like I do with ADHD or find it hard to focus, start small. I suggest reading fifteen minutes a day, uninterrupted. It's a great way to build the habit. Later, you can add a few minutes each week. In no time, you'll be reading thirty minutes a day, and then an hour. Time and again, this incremental-step technique has proven to be a valuable way to make time my friend. It can be applied to just about anything you want to learn or do more of. Start with small increments. Then increase the time just a little each week until you hit your stride—the best amount of daily time to produce the best results.

The reason I started reading so much was an article I stumbled upon a few years back that said the average CEO reads close to a book a week. Then I looked up how much the average person reads and was quite surprised. It was only one to three books a year. Since 2017, I have stayed consistent with my goal to read one book per week. I have found this habit to be life changing and very rewarding. It has helped me continually improve as a life coach, athlete, and parent.

Not every book I read turns out to be a gold mine of information. But I haven't regretted any book that I have read. Each one either teaches me something new or helps me relearn or reinforce a valuable lesson.

SOCIAL MEDIA: FRIEND OR FOE?

Social media can be great if we use it wisely to educate ourselves, but if we don't, it can be a crutch. Let's be conservative and say you only spend twenty minutes a day on your lunch break scrolling through your feed and looking at people's stories. That doesn't seem like a lot, but over a seven-day week, it adds up to a little over nine hours a month. Think about what you could be doing with that time.

Let's extend that out even further. Twenty minutes a day for a year adds up to roughly 120 hours. If you devoted that time to taking college-level courses, you'd be well on your way to a degree. It's not just about how we use the 120 hours—it's about the habit of better time management and what we could gain, instead of lose, with our time. What if the time you normally spend on Instagram were spent instead on looking at content that serves you? Maybe looking up people who are motivators and could help your business. Or, if you're into fitness, checking out some workout tips. Or, if you like cooking, interfacing with a chef who creates tasty food recipes. Think about it. There's mindless internet content that amounts to fluff, and there's mindful internet content that can pay dividends in one's future.

Turning off social media notifications will help you control that quick-fix dopamine hit you've become used to receiving. Unless I am expecting something important (a reply to a question I asked, for instance), I make a point to check my email only a couple of times a day. And each day, I go on social media and make all of my business-related posts at once instead of sporadically throughout the day. Be vigilant, be disciplined, and use your free time to learn rather than to browse through endless videos of cute cats and dogs.

BUSINESS LUNCH VERSUS BS LUNCH

A large time waster for me in the past was doing things I didn't want to just to please others. These days, I don't waste valuable time having coffee or lunch with people just because they asked me to and I don't want to hurt their feelings by saying no. That's not to say I never go out for lunch or coffee. I'm just selective with the company I keep, as I have a wife and a child I'm responsible for, plus a supplement company and coaching business to run. So if someone I know is bored and wants to kill time by shooting the bull over coffee, I have no problem saying, "Sorry—can't afford the time." For years, I allowed people to push and pull me in all directions, and I ended up overworked, overwhelmed, and burnt out. On the other hand, if someone wants to have a productive lunch talking business strategy, that will be time well spent.

YOUR THOUGHTS: FRIEND OR FOE?

Our thoughts can either be our best friends or our worst enemies. Years ago, I heard someone say they never let people rent space in their head. I thought that was such a great saying, and it really stuck with me.

Have you ever thought about all the time we waste on negative thoughts? We complain and moan over things that don't go our way or as planned. We overstress constantly about the future—I like to call this "future-tripping." And we spend so much time worrying about how we look to the world and are constantly trying to please others.

We don't need to do any of this.

I've had clients say to me, "But Mike, sometimes I can't help it. Sometimes I'm bombarded by negative thoughts as if they have a will of their own. What do I do when that happens?"

I tell them, "It's easier than you think to turn it around and get back to positive thinking. Just use the STOP or STAMP techniques I taught you."

This will work for you as well. When negative thoughts start attacking, head them off at the pass with STOP or STAMP. Use these techniques to get back on track fast with positive thinking.

TV: FRIEND OR FOE?

How much time do you spend watching reality TV programs? How much value is there in watching people argue over nothing? Reality TV is addicting because it's pure entertainment and doesn't require us to think. It's easy to look at other people's problems to avoid our own.

If you are hooked on watching nonstop reality TV, here is something that can help. Just like with junk food, consuming it in small doses and on occasion is okay—but it's not healthy for every meal. My wife loves to binge-watch the various *Housewives* series, and when she asks me to join her, I'll watch one episode. And I do it without judgement. One off-diet meal a week is not going to ruin your life. Start by cutting down on the reality episodes, and then replace them with shows on the Discovery, National Geographic, and History channels.

While watching educational TV, I keep a pen and pad on the coffee table and will occasionally jot down a piece of information that I can use later to improve some aspect of my life—for example, the name of a scientist, researcher, or whoever whose book I want to be sure to read.

THE INTERNET: FRIEND OR FOE?

Too many people I know are caught up in aimlessly surfing the internet strictly for entertainment. Being bored and surfing the internet as an outlet wastes more precious hours than we realize.

I remember when YouTube first came out; I'd get lost in watching goofy videos for hours and put off important business matters that needed my attention.

If you are working on a difficult task and feel yourself drifting, instead of surfing the web, turn the computer off, get up, and do something that's physical for ten to fifteen minutes. If I find myself losing focus in the middle of a project, I'll take my dog for a ten-minute walk. Or I'll do push-ups and sit-ups, jump rope, or shadowbox—anything as a respite to get the blood flowing and get me back on track.

Do you abandon your projects in favor of other people's pages? Some people can spend hours trolling other people's content for a fun fix, which serves no purpose. Just recently, a couple friends of mine went at it for two hours on my Instagram profile over something I posted. I messaged them both privately and told them I was deleting the post. I have made it a habit to delete negative comments on my posts and not engage. If someone has nothing nice to say, that's on them; I just delete the comment and move on.

BEDTIME: FRIEND OR FOE?

Are you one of those people who stay up well past midnight simply because you're not ready to sleep yet? Or, when the day is over, do you lie in bed awake at night, mulling over how your day went? Nighttime is the time to reset and get your mind and body ready for the next day. Don't waste it by ruminating when you could be recharging. A solid seven to eight hours of sleep is so important to our health.

Unfortunately, I have a lot of clients who have trouble sleeping. After their heads hit the pillow, their minds are still running nonstop.

How we end our day is just as important as how we start it. Learning to unwind correctly will help you get a restful night of sleep.

Even though some evenings I have to be on calls with clients, I inform people that I'm shutting down my phone ninety minutes before I go to bed, which is generally in the vicinity of 8:30 PM.

In the evening, I make sure not to watch anything too intense, like a murder mystery or a horror movie—otherwise, I can't sleep. I don't look at emails or text messages after 8 PM. And I never eat any high-carbohydrate or sugar-filled foods after 7 PM. On nights when I am "wired," I take supplements such as magnesium, melatonin, and valerian root, which I have found relax me in the evening. Also, reading a half-hour before lights-out or playing calming music helps me relax and fall asleep more easily.

RELATIONSHIPS: FRIEND OR FOE?

Holding onto relationships that add no meaning or value to who we are is another potential time killer. We have to remove the Anchors: people that bring zero value to our lives. For me, this has been something I've constantly had to work on. In the past, I have held onto draining relationships for far too long—costing me not only time but also a lot of money. I have since learned not to be swayed by someone's palaver. Instead, I pay attention to their actions. I look at how they treat others and what their daily routine and habits are like.

Over the years, my values have changed—and with them, the company I keep. Being sober and getting up at 4 AM isn't going to work when surrounded by people who drink all night and into the morning. Now I look at my life and goals and work out whether the relationships I have fit into that picture. I have outgrown a lot of people, and that's okay. I never try to change people and convince them they need to be more like me. I just walk away.

Arguing with Friends, Family, and Loved Ones

Arguing over things that we can't change is absolutely pointless and serves zero purpose. Focusing on what we *can* change is all we can do. For example, if the weather is bad, can I change it? If I'm driving down the highway and someone cuts me off, can I change it? The only thing I'm in full control of is my response, not what people do or say to me.

I've learned the hard way over the years that trying to change people is a fool's errand and a complete waste of energy. We all have our own opinions, and we don't have to all agree. I have found it's more productive to meet people where they're at and to let go of any judgment. Even when I'm coaching a client, I never try to change them. I listen to them and do my best to look at their world from how they see it. Then I suggest things that may help them solve a problem or make a better choice—from their perspective, not mine.

I was working with a client recently (who I'll call Jack) who was really struggling with the concept of same-sex marriage. Jack was fighting constantly with his friends over it and even had three lifetime friends stop talking to him over his views.

I personally don't have an issue with same-sex marriage. How other people choose to live their lives is not my concern. When Jack and I first met to talk, I allowed him to open up about why he didn't agree with the concept. He explained that he had a very strong religious upbringing and had been told all his life it was a sin and went against God for two people of the same sex to be married.

Now, I didn't have a very strong religious upbringing. I did grow up in a small town with narrow-minded people, but I never really allowed them to affect my views.

Knowing we had different views on the subject, I had to hear his perspective without judgment. I allowed Jack to express why he thought it was wrong. I didn't try to change his opinion; I just listened.

Then I told him, "I can understand your point of view. Whether I agree with it or not, it's your beliefs and principles based on what you believe."

Once Jack was relaxed and no longer defensive, I asked him a simple question: "Does it actually affect you *personally* if two people of the same sex get married?"

Jack gave this some thought, then admitted that he was "old school" and didn't like the concept but could see how it didn't actually affect him in any way. And while he felt that same-sex marriage violated one of his values, he understood that it wasn't his place to try and control people and that he'd get along better with his liberal friends if he were less judgmental. It's been slow going, but day by day, as Jack moves away from judging others for their beliefs and choices and instead uses that time to focus on himself, he is becoming more productive.

To follow are some techniques I have used to maximize my time:

KNOW WHAT YOU WANT AND WHY YOU WANT IT

Like I talked about in chapter five on having a purpose, I find my life becomes a lot easier when I know *why* I am doing something. And keeping that "why" at the forefront of my mind—or reminding myself of it when I start to drift—is a powerful motivating factor.

Every day, I focus on bringing value to other people—motivating, educating, and inspiring them to live their best lives. As long as I'm making sure to do those three things, I can easily forgo or ignore the temptation to procrastinate or dawdle.

START YOUR DAY EARLY

I get up early (usually between 3:30 and 4:30 AM) and own my morning. Peace and quiet, no interruptions—it's been life changing. I can get so much done before 8 AM, when most people are just getting out of bed. I have actually closed business deals at 5 AM because I know a lot of like-minded people who love the early morning for getting things done.

WORK SMARTER, NOT HARDER

A common problem that pops up with clients who come to me for business coaching is inefficiency. They spend a lot of effort for little return. I start by looking at how they plan their day (unfortunately, some don't plan at all).

I tell them: "Let's say I have six tasks to complete today. Which one do I attack first? Second, third, etc.? The answer is *never* 'the easiest one.' It's the one that is going to bring me the most return for the time I spend on it. And so on, down the line."

This is not so much about efficiency as it is about analysis of time investment versus return. But in terms of efficiency, I am always looking at how I can do less and accomplish more. And the solutions are almost always . . .

- Eliminate time wasters (as I've discussed throughout this chapter).
- Do the hardest tasks first, except when they have little payoff.
- Work from a plan that I wrote the night before instead of winging it.

- Separate priorities from options.
- Work smart as opposed to working quickly (e.g., look for opportunities where I can multitask).

PLAN YOUR DAY IN DETAIL AND STICK TO IT

I break my day into three parts.

1. Mike Time: 3 to 8 AM
2. Work Time: 8 AM to 6 PM
3. Family and Fun Time: 6 to 9 PM

Mike Time is all about me. Yes, me. My mental and physical health.

During this time, I meditate, work out, read, write, and work on creative projects. Mike Time goes from Monday to Sunday. I don't take days off with my meditation and exercise. I don't find meditating and working out to be chores. I love doing them. I'll never trade my early mornings for the all-night schedule I used to have. I can't be my best if I don't discipline myself this way.

Work Time goes Monday to Friday. On the weekends, I do my best not to schedule clients, but sometimes with my sobriety coaching clients I have to be flexible. During Work Time, I do my Zoom coaching calls, weekly podcasts, marketing for Diamond Life Fuel, and content creation.

I break my clients into two groups: sobriety coaching, and life and business coaching. I prioritize them accordingly. My clients who need sobriety coaching take precedence over business clients right now, as they are at higher risk. I don't work hourly anymore. All my clients pay monthly retainers, and we preschedule our meetings for each month. I have found that by doing this, it keeps not only my clients disciplined but also myself. I maintain eight clients a month, and I'm super strict with them. I lay down the foundation of what needs to be done based on their goals. If they don't stick to the plan, I move on to the next person on my waiting list. When I first started coaching, I wasn't this disciplined and allowed my clients to control my day. I soon got burnt out trying to please everyone. But now I have a set daily regimen and am able to get twice as much done as before.

When it comes to Family and Fun Time, with COVID-19 and lockdown, going out isn't always an option. I usually leave it up to my wife what we do at home. But I still put a limit on TV time. Sometimes we play interactive games, which has brought us closer as a family. Family and Fun Time has quelled my tendency to be a round-the-clock workaholic, which keeps everyone happy—myself included.

PREPARE LUNCH MEALS IN ADVANCE

I spend a part of my Sundays cooking healthy lunch meals for the week, and this has been a game changer. Before I started prepping my lunch meals, I'd often give in to the urge to eat fast food to get by. In the past, eating junk food always affected my weight and moods, slowing me down. Now, just two hours on a Sunday sets up my week perfectly. I either freeze or refrigerate everything, and the meals go straight into the microwave and are ready to go when I want to eat. I make my breakfast at 10 AM, usually consisting of oatmeal and eggs (healthy, plus quick and easy to cook). And I almost always have dinner with my family.

Now, if you're not a good cook, or if you just don't like cooking, there is nothing wrong with having something like Healthy Choice meals on hand. But be careful not to get pre-made meals that are loaded with carbohydrates, saturated fats, and sugars. I always look at the labels and read the ingredients before I buy.

If you don't mind spending a little extra money, there are several companies that prepare and deliver nutritious meals to you. This can help you avoid snacking on a bag of chips and drinking high-sugar soda drinks from the vending machine for lunch.

I also suggest that you not eat your lunch at your desk. Take a minimum of thirty minutes to eat something healthy in peace and quiet. I ate on the run for years, and it really affected my performance—besides giving me horrible stomach issues. I also recommend eating meals slowly. I used to wolf down food like I was in an eating contest and never felt satisfied afterwards. You will be much more productive throughout the afternoon by making these small adjustments.

USE SOCIAL MEDIA PRIMARILY FOR BUSINESS AND *OCCASIONALLY* FOR PLEASURE

Unfortunately, for many people, this rule is the reverse, with social media used primarily for pleasure. It was a tough habit for me to change, but well worth it. I used to spend hours on Instagram and Facebook. Now I only post a few stories that are relevant to my supplement company and coaching business. I keep it simple and don't overdo it. I usually do my social media posts at the end of my workday after I've taken care of my top business priorities. I do respond to people who message me, but only after the priority projects are completed.

CHECK EMAILS ONLY TWICE A DAY

I do this after I do my morning meditation, reading, stretching, and workout.

Some self-help experts will tell you, "Only check your email once a day, and *never* in the morning—only at the end of the day." The problem for most of us is that, often, important business emails arrive in the early morning and contain matters that need to be addressed immediately. I read those emails in the morning and postpone the nonimportant ones for the end of the day.

MEDITATE TWICE A DAY

This has helped me manage my stress and has especially helped me overcome not only my short-fused temper but also my ulcerative colitis. Doing deep breathwork has really slowed me down in a good way. My racing mind is now more focused—hence, more productive. But even if you meditate only once a day, it will still have amazing results.

Meditation first thing in the morning kick-starts my day. Then a shorter meditation in the early afternoon recharges me. Because I get up so early, sometimes I can get burnt out by 4 PM. This second meditation also helps me stay present for my family duties.

GO TO SLEEP AT THE SAME TIME EVERY NIGHT

Sleep is so vital to how we function. Sleep deprivation can affect our memory, ability to focus, mood, and health. There is a reason why in most special forces training they deprive new recruits of sleep. It is the quickest way to get the recruits to a state of maximum stress so they can see how they hold up under pressure. It's very hard to function at our best when we aren't well rested.

A study published in *BMC Public Health* in 2009 on college students in Taiwan found that irregular bedtimes left students tossing and turning all night, which isn't great given that sleep deprivation can affect how we perform under pressure.

In 2010, SRI International studied eight thousand four-year-old children around the United States. The researchers found that when the children had consistent bedtime rules, they scored better in language, math, and literacy tests.

Irregular sleeping affects our circadian rhythms, which can throw our body clocks out of whack. If you have ever traveled overseas or across several time zones, you have probably experienced jet lag. But some people actually get what's called "social jet lag." This occurs when people have regular sleep habits during the week but party hard until all hours of the morning on the weekends.

Once I disciplined myself to go to bed at the same time every night and wake up at the same time every morning, getting a good night's sleep was no longer a problem. I rarely use an alarm clock these days, as my body clock knows when to sleep and when to wake up.

A few years ago, I stumbled upon on a theory known as the Pareto principle in a Forbes article that I've found to be very useful.[12] Vilfredo Pareto was an Italian engineer, sociologist, economist, political scientist, and philosopher. He observed that 80 percent of the wealth in Italy belonged to just 20 percent of the population. The Pareto principle argues that about 80 percent of consequences come from only about 20 percent of causes—hence why the principle is also called the "80/20 rule." The more I read about this principle, the more it made me think about and observe the world around me and the importance of quality over quantity.

It also got me thinking about spending the right amount of time and effort on things that can help me get closer to achieving my goals and purpose on a day-to-day basis. The Pareto principle can be very effective in teaching us how to prioritize our time effectively. Spend the right 20 percent of quality time, or get 20 percent of the right people around you, and you should get a disproportionately large return.

I mean, it makes a lot of sense. We shouldn't spend major time on minor things that bring us no value. Like they say, we are the company we keep. If you hang out with five drunks, you will be the sixth. If you hang out with five successful millionaires, you will be the sixth. Essentially, good people in the right places can help raise the standard for everyone.

This principle is very evident when it comes to sports teams. Players like Michael Jordan, Lebron James, and Kobe Bryant are known for carrying their teams. Great quarterbacks are the same. Tom Brady is the perfect example. Brady is so good and so dangerous that even with just a few seconds left on the clock, he can win the game if he gets the ball in his hands.

Years ago, when I was living in New York City, I remember going to Yankee Stadium to watch the Yankees take on the Arizona Diamondbacks. I was so excited to see the Yankees play that day. They had an incredible lineup, with players like Derek Jeter, Alex Rodriguez, and Jason Giambi. But that all changed when Hall of Famer Randy Johnson stepped up to pitch. Nicknamed "The Big Unit," Johnson ripped through the Yankees' lineup like a hot knife through warm butter, and the Yankees were barely able to register a single hit.

The point of the Pareto principle is to make sure we place our focus and attention on the things that can produce the most reward and value for any project or goal we are working towards achieving.

So, you may be wondering: "How has Mike Diamond applied the Pareto principle in his own life?"

I always start by setting a measurable goal. Then I work backwards to plot out the most effective and time-efficient way to proceed.

I applied the Pareto principle when I competed in my first men's physique contest. My goal was to make it to the Natural Olympia competition in the shortest time possible. The first thing I did was look up which federation held the Natural Olympia contest. I found out that it was the International Natural Bodybuilding Association. Once I knew that, I looked to see if I knew anyone who'd competed with the organization before.

To my surprise, my friend Dan Zigler had already competed in multiple contests for the same association. Perfect! Dan's my guy, then. I called Dan, and he told me all I had to do was win two shows in twelve months to qualify for the Natural Olympia contest. I found out there where two shows on the same day in Las Vegas, twelve weeks away. The Natural Olympia contest was six weeks after that.

Next, I came up with a twelve-week program to compete. I trained for ninety days straight, dieted hard, and competed in a natural Men's Physique bodybuilding competition hosted by the INBA/PNBA. I took first place in the Masters category (ages 40–49), and on the same day competed in the Men's Novice competition, which was open to all ages, where I placed second out of ten contestants. That ranking qualified me to compete in the Natural Mr. Olympia competition. I trained for six more weeks and ended up taking a bronze medal in the Over 45 INBA/PNBA Natural Olympia Men's Physique Show.

It was only my third contest in just under four months, whereas most people take *years* to compete in one show. Dan was my 20 percent. All of his experience gave me the blueprint and the laser-focus I needed to achieve my goal. It saved me months of arbitrary training on a wing and a prayer.

I opened my supplement company, Diamond Life Fuel, using the same principle. I didn't try selling hundreds of products with the hope that at least some of them would succeed. Instead, I did my research (the 20 percent) and created an ingredient I knew would work. I had sampled so many supplements while healing myself naturally from my ulcerative colitis that I was able to narrow them down to a select few I was confident in.

I called my friend Sam, who owns a supplement company, and told him my idea. He asked me, "Do you have an ingredient?" I said yes, and he said, "Let's send it to my lab."

In less than sixty days, a sample was ready. We tested the sample repeatedly. It both tasted great and made us feel great.

I like to say, "Your network is your net worth." Sam was an integral part of my 20 percent. I always go to people who have more experience and knowledge than me to help me get started. Having the right people with the right contacts and network is invaluable.

Even when I lift weights, I choose the basic exercises that challenge me the most and stick to them. Pull-ups, push-ups, squats, and good old-fashioned dips. Then cardio is either running, hiking, or cycling.

When I was working in the nightclub security business, I needed to make sure I could protect myself and subdue people when I needed to. I went straight to a Navy SEAL friend and asked him to teach me five key moves to make sure I could take care of myself: an arm bar, a standing chokehold, two takedowns, and a wrist lock was all I ever needed to get the job done.

So you can see how I take the idea of the Pareto principle and put my own spin on it. I'm always thinking about how to get the most value out of the least amount of time and effort. When you are seeking top quality, you need all 100 percent. When you are trying to optimize the most bang for your buck, focusing on the critical 20 percent is a time saver. Treat time with care, and it will become one of your best friends.

Chapter 9

FINALIZE YOUR PLAN FOR SUCCESS WITH SELF-DISCIPLINE AND SPIRITUALITY

Years ago, I heard a story that really hit me deep. It involves discipline, and it changed my life.

Two twin boys, who I'll call Tom and Dick, were living with their father, Harry, in the inner city. One night, after he put the boys to bed, Harry got into an argument with his neighbor. It was late, and Harry had already downed a few drinks after a brutal sixteen-hour shift. The neighbor wouldn't turn down his stereo, and Harry, not thinking clearly, decided to threaten him with a gun to get him to "Turn that damn thing off!"

It's been said that every second of the day, we are all just one decision away from a disempowering or an empowering choice. And the ripple effect of an empowering or disempowering choice can last a lifetime.

During the ensuing scuffle, the gun went off, and Harry accidentally killed the neighbor. Harry went to prison; the boys were put into the foster care system and became separated. Going forward, each boy made completely different life choices. Dick did not apply himself and did poorly in school. Several truancies led to being expelled. At age fourteen, Dick lost his temper and killed a foster sibling in an argument over a TV remote control.

The other boy, Tom, did well in school. He always got his homework assignments done on time. He practiced hard and excelled in sports. Tom also did volunteer work in his community and became a positive influence in society.

One of the boys had big dreams for his future; the other lived moment to moment, reacting on impulse to situations that confronted him.

By the age of twenty-four, now adults, they had made completely different life choices. Dick was in jail serving multiple life sentences. Tom had graduated magna cum laude from an Ivy League college and was about to begin work at a tech company. He was also ready to get married and start a family.

Both were interviewed, and what I found interesting was that even though Dick and Tom had taken completely different paths, they both had the same answer to one question. It was a simple question but a powerful one: "What caused you to make the choices you've made up to this point in your life?"

As I said, both boys had the same answer. Although their words were slightly different, in essence they both said: "Do you know who my dad was? Well, what choice did I have?"

We all have a past with elements of both good and bad. And that past can make us either victims or victors depending on the choices we make along the way and on the commitment we make to favor and uphold our higher or better self. The story we tell ourselves over and over again is much more powerful than the story others tell us.

Now, some people may presume that Dick must have had bad foster parents and that Tom didn't. Whether or not that was the case, it still doesn't change the fact that each one of us gets to choose how we think, feel, and act in every situation that presents itself to us.

I see this all the time when I do interventions. Some kids come from nothing and still make the best of it. Other kids have it all and blow every opportunity. The point of the story and countless other similar stories is to show us the power of focusing on the positive and making empowering choices no matter where we come from or which cards we are dealt.

From my perspective, the most obvious trait separating those who succeed from those who fail is self-discipline.

As exemplified by Tom, it is essential to have the discipline to cultivate positive habits and push through the hard times. In order to master your life in all areas, you must develop discipline—because self-discipline is the starting line for success.

HABITS OF SELF-DISCIPLINED PEOPLE

1. SELF-DISCIPLINED PEOPLE DELAY GRATIFICATION

Deciding not to take the easy route almost always leads to major gains and much more pleasure than you could have had with instant gratification. But it's not simple to do, as we all know. Maintaining discipline can seem overwhelming at times, with so many tempting options and distractions constantly bombarding our senses.

For example, let's say you are working on an important project on your computer. It's getting tough. You're getting tired. And right there in your browser's "Favorites" bookmark, YouTube, Facebook, Instagram, etc., are beckoning you. Or maybe your favorite computer game, *Minecraft*, *Fortnite*, or *Grand Theft Auto*, is winking at you. How tempting it is to bail for an hour or two and indulge in some fun.

When people talk about delaying gratification, what they are saying is: "I discipline myself to resist the immediate reward of a small, short-term, pleasurable experience in exchange for a much bigger reward in the future."

Even though that package of cookies is tempting now—and will surely taste good—by delaying that pleasure, we can get the six-pack abs we desire in the future.

There was a famous series of experiments done at Stanford University popularly known today as the "Marshmallow Test."[13] In 1972, psychologist Walter Mischel and his team tested hundreds of children, mostly between the ages of four and five. The experiments were very simple and would test to see if children could delay gratification. Simply put, in one experiment, a researcher would offer children two options: one treat (like a pretzel) right away, or a more desired treat (like a marshmallow) if they had the patience to delay the gratification and wait for fifteen minutes. Pretty simple, right? Wait out the fifteen minutes and boom—you get a better treat. But the research team added a little catch: they placed the treats on the table in front of the toddlers and then walked out the room, leaving the toddlers all alone with the snacks right in front of them. Now, I don't know about you, but even I have trouble some days resisting temptation, so for a toddler, this really was a test. Unbeknownst to the toddlers, the researchers sat back in another room and observed their struggle.

According to Mischel, some of the kids jumped up to eat the treats as soon as the researcher left the room. Other kids bounced around, trying to distract themselves. Only a small handful of children had the discipline to resist the immediate reward.

So did delaying the instant gratification to receive more marshmallows really matter? Well, apparently it did. Years after the initial marshmallow experiment was conducted at Stanford, Mischel and his team tracked down the kids to see how they were doing in their lives, and what they discovered was quite interesting. The kids who were able to wait longest in the experiment had higher SAT scores, were better at handling high levels of stress, and had better social skills when compared to the other participants. Experiments like this have been conducted over the years to assess the benefits of people's ability to delay gratification.

As a kid, I could never delay gratification. I always felt that I was never going to get enough. I wanted my fix *now*! I had no faith in a promising future or trust in the reliability of others. Consequently, I started experimenting with drugs and alcohol in my early teen years because I felt I could trust the instant reward. And that was why I relied on drugs for so many years and why my life seemed to always be a constant struggle.

This went on until I finally dug deeper than I ever thought possible and made the decision to get and stay sober. Eliminating my need for instant gratification precluded the possibility of relapsing. Over the fifteen years since, my self-discipline of delayed gratification has allowed me to build a wildly successful coaching and speaking career. And this has led to a highly gratifying lifestyle that I now enjoy each and every day.

In working with addicts over the years, I've seen that this self-discipline in delaying gratification is the one thing they all struggle with and have to master if they want to remain sober. But it's not just addicts who struggle with this. No one gets a pass when it comes to avoiding the trap of taking a shortcut or seeking a quick fix of pleasure.

When I'm coaching clients, I start with two simple steps to help them build this effective habit.

STEP ONE: I tell my clients to create some long-term goals that will bring them pleasure in the future—something big in terms of a reward to look forward to. Something as simple as wanting to purchase a new car can help you control your mindless spending now and save daily for your future goal. You could create weight-loss goals or start fitness challenges, like running a 5K or half-marathon. Or you could start a course online to further your education or complete the education you never got around to in your earlier years. Even taking up martial arts is an amazing way to develop self-discipline.

When I first got sober, I went back to study Kyokushin karate. I'd studied this type of karate as a kid, but I hated the grading system and soon bailed. Going back as an adult gave me a whole different perspective and respect for the art. And the self-discipline it required paid off in spades.

All these goals have a *target* in sight, which will help you stay the course. Creating forward motivation is crucial in keeping you on track.

STEP TWO: Take things one step at a time and celebrate the small victories. For example, after a hard week of training, treat yourself to a soothing massage or a satisfying meal. Now, when I say "satisfying meal," I don't mean a whole pizza or three In-N-Out burgers with fries. One scoop of your favorite ice cream or a couple slices of pizza is okay, though.

When I was training for the Natural Olympia Men's Physique contest, I'd wait all week to have one cheat meal. It was usually a burger, and I didn't order fries. Then I'd go back to my regular strict diet protocol until the next week. My point is, don't overdo your celebration reward, or you will be back at square one.

I always tell clients that if your goal is to lose a desired amount of weight, start with removing one high-caloric food you know needs to be eliminated from your diet. Then add a little bit of cardio, like walking twenty minutes a day. I have found that people who go at it too hard too fast end up sore, tired, or feeling lousy and then become disgruntled with completing the goal—because there is no enjoyment of the process whatsoever. It becomes all pain and zero gain.

When you celebrate the small victories, you slowly build new, positive habits and find it easier to discipline yourself with more empowering choices. Soon, delaying gratification will become an enjoyable habit.

2. SELF-DISCIPLINED PEOPLE HAVE SELF-CONTROL

You hear people talk about self-control, self-awareness, the importance of living in the present moment, and being in control of our emotions. But what does it really mean to have self-control? To me, self-control is the ability to take charge of my emotions, calculate my actions (rather than blindly reacting), and, in the end, take responsibility for my choices. Reacting and responding are two different things. When we *react*, we are operating out of our primitive brains in survival mode. When we *respond*, we have first processed the situation we are dealing with and are then acting accordingly—in our best interests as well as in the best interests of others.

Building self-control takes time, but anyone can do it. A strong sense of self-control makes it easier to be more self-disciplined. And here's how:

STEP ONE: Start taking inventory of your thoughts and feelings daily. Notice when you are reacting versus when you are responding. In the beginning, it will be helpful to keep a journal and note when you are doing one or the other. Consciously reducing your reacting and increasing your responding will make you self-aware and allow you to see when and where you go off track with the choices you are making.

Taking inventory will also help you process your thoughts and emotions. Stop and reflect on *why* you reacted to something. Notice how a pause would assist you in thinking more clearly, allowing you to respond rather than react next time. Learning to control our thoughts and emotions won't happen unless we are aware of what we think and feel.

Unfortunately, some people believe they have no choice in how they feel. When I coach, I hear certain people insist, "This is the way I was born" or "My bad temper is genetic. I inherited it from my dad/mom." Some people blame their culture or upbringing for their lack of restraint and control in challenging situations. For example, there is the infamous "Irish temper" that some people of that heritage claim they are saddled with. But for every hothead, I can point to another Irish person who rarely loses their temper. Those people have *chosen* not to be a victim of their circumstances—or, more specifically, a victim of their cultural stereotype.

Here's the deal: none of these types of beliefs is actually true—unless you buy into them. We can all have better self-control and master our emotions and actions if we are willing to take responsibility and have the self-discipline to do the work by taking inventory.

STEP TWO: Breathe. Yes, there's that word again: breathe. I've said it before, but it bears repeating. When you're freaked-out angry, instead of counting to ten, take ten deep breaths. This will get you calmer and cooler faster. And it will put you in a state of mind to intelligently deal with the challenge you face.

STEP THREE: Practice the STOP and STAMP methods I introduced in chapter three. These are two amazing techniques to help you gain more self-control. Remember: anything important takes time, but with practice, we get better. And practice is cumulative. The more you practice, the faster you adapt. And eventually, you reach a tipping point (thank you, Malcolm Gladwell) where less is more. That is, you reach a stage where a small amount of practice produces bigger results than ever before.

3. SELF-DISCIPLINED PEOPLE SET MACRO AND MICRO GOALS

There is a famous saying: "Dreams without goals are just dreams."

Early on in life, I had goals, but I didn't really understand the process of micro and macro goal setting. We need to have both kinds if we want to succeed. Self-disciplined people understand the importance of setting realistic goals.

Macro goals are the big-picture ones. They create the target we want to hit, the destination we want to arrive at. Micro goals are the nitty-gritty steps we take along the way to close the gap from where we are to where we want to be. Goal setting helps us become accountable and focused on what we want.

STEP ONE: Write down three to five things you want to achieve in the next year. Now ask yourself these questions in this order:

"Why do I want to achieve these goals?"
It's important to know your "why." This will give you ongoing motivation and help you stay on track to see your goals through the end.

"How will I get started?"
We have to start somewhere. Getting started is what I find most people get stuck with. I hear it all the time with my clients: "I have all these ideas, but I just don't know where to start." Get yourself out of indecision by just choosing *something* as a starting point. If necessary, you can make small adjustments as you go.

"What steps do I need to take?"
Here is the power of the micro goal process. By breaking things down and lining them up, you can create a realistic set of actions and habits to get you going. This way, you won't feel overwhelmed.

"Has it been done before?"
I know we all feel our ideas are one in a million, but the truth is that someone has probably already done something similar. That isn't necessarily a bad thing, though, so don't let this discourage you. Use the information their example provides and model their behavior. But be sure to put your own special twist on it. People use this strategy all the time, and it's highly effective, as long as you are not infringing on someone else's copyright or patent.

Now, once you have the major target in mind, work backwards to monthly, weekly, and daily targets. If they don't line up, then the goals aren't realistic.

It's great to want big things and set high goals, but our actions have to match our intentions, or those goals just aren't going to happen. Like they say, you have to walk the talk.

STEP TWO: Find a mentor or someone to hold you accountable. Having a person hold you accountable (to hitting your micro goals) who you can also talk to or brainstorm with will be more valuable than you can imagine.

Do not get discouraged and throw in the towel when something doesn't go exactly as planned. Maybe the universe is trying to tell you there's a better plan than your original one—if only you resist thinking defeatist thoughts and are open to possibility. This is where having a mentor has been invaluable to me. Many times, bouncing ideas off a mentor and getting a different perspective has sent me on a new course that turned out much better than I initially planned for.

I always go to a mentor who has more experience than me when I'm attempting to achieve a major goal. Don't give up if you can't find someone right away. You will if you keep looking. Don't be afraid to pick up the phone and call people or email them. I do it all the time.

Before I made the cover of *Recovery Today* magazine, I emailed the owner of the magazine multiple times, even though he kept putting me off with "Maybe some other time." I was so persistent, he finally gave me an interview. Then I simply asked, "Who is set for the cover story?" Rob, the owner, was honest and said, "We have someone else slated." I replied, "No problem. Can't hurt to ask." Two weeks later, I received a phone call from Rob: "Hey, Michael. The guest we had for that issue just pulled out. Would you like to be on the cover?"

Life is short. Ask for what you want. You may be surprised at the result.

4. SELF-DISCIPLINED PEOPLE OWN THE MORNING AND HAVE DAILY RITUALS

Top athletes, entrepreneurs, and entertainers alike have talked about the importance of starting the day early with empowering rituals. I have followed the Navy SEALs, who swear by waking up at 5 AM to start the day. But it's not just the early start that's important when creating self-discipline—it's the actions we take that become our daily habits. For me, it's meditation, stretching, lifting weights, reading, journaling, running, and taking cold showers. I keep this regimen very strict. That way, the rest of the day is easy for me. The way you start the day will affect the course of your day. Either you own the day, or the day owns you.

STEP ONE: No more snooze button. Set a time to get up and stick to it each day—no matter how you feel. The earlier, the better. Wash your face with cold water or take a cold shower. Yes, a cold shower. It won't kill you; trust me on this. It will wake you up and prime you for taking action.

Then, read something positive and uplifting. I read for a minimum of thirty minutes in the morning. It helps clear my mind and fills me with information that I often find helps me later in the day. Like they say: information in, information out.

I suggest you start by reading for a minimum of fifteen minutes. At first, you might say, "It's just fifteen minutes. What's that going to do?" Well, as the famous saying goes, don't knock it till you've tried it! I'm betting you'll be so surprised at the results, you'll start looking forward to reading each morning, too.

There are tons of inspirational and educational books to choose from. Start with one that relates to your field or interests. These three books are some of my top recommendations for anyone who is looking to improve themselves and live a better life: *Think and Grow Rich* by Napoleon Hill (I feel it's a timeless gem), *Grit* by Angela Duckworth, and *Emotional Intelligence* by Daniel Goleman. These three books will really help you kick-start your day.

It's important not to read emails when you first wake up. Reading something positive instead will help set a good tone for the rest of the day.

Some people prefer audiobooks, which I also love. When I have an exceptionally busy day ahead of me, sometimes I'll use an audiobook to multitask. I'll put on my headphones and listen while stretching or lifting weights. Just try it—you might like it!

Next, write down three things you are grateful for. You'll be surprised how well this works. Being grateful for what you already have sets you up to attract what you don't have but strongly desire. Don't ask me how that works. Just give it a shot. Millions of people have and are immensely glad they did. And remember to be grateful for even the small things. This promotes and reinforces a positive, optimistic outlook to start the day before we start grinding away.

Do at least twenty minutes of exercise. I personally like circuit training, cardio, and cross-training, like P90X or Insanity. This gets the heart pumping, the blood flowing, and the endorphins jumping.

Then sit quietly for five to ten minutes and visualize the day before it happens. I'm big on playing a positive movie over and over in my mind.

STEP TWO: Eat a solid breakfast with protein, carbs, and healthy fats. Even though I fast for sixteen hours a day, I still eat a few carbs in the morning after I train. It helps with my moods and cravings so that I don't feel the urge to snack on junk foods.

These simple but basic habits are most effective when performed at the same time in the same order at the start of each day. They will really help you get going and feel good throughout the rest of your day.

Years ago, when I used to get home and go to bed around 4 AM, if someone had told me that one day that I'd love the idea of waking up around that time, I would've told them they were out of their mind. But now I love getting up early and owning the day.

5. SELF-DISCIPLINED PEOPLE KNOW THE IMPORTANCE OF MANAGING TIME

With the same twenty-four hours in each day, why is it that some people get so much done while others always seem to be behind and chasing their tails? Which one are you? Do you always seem to be playing catch-up? Or do you control the day and your schedule?

Self-disciplined people understand the value of time. And they do not waste it on trivial matters.

If you feel you occasionally waste time or get pulled in all directions, here are two steps that can help you manage your time more effectively.

STEP ONE: Know what matters most to you and why. Knowing what really matters helps you spend time on tasks that get you closer to what you want. For example, I don't waste time binge-watching TV shows. I'll sit down and watch one episode of a series each night—but never three or four episodes in one day. Instead, I'll spend an hour or so reading a book, fiction or nonfiction, that expands my knowledge.

I'm the same with the time I spend with the company I keep. I thoroughly like to be around people. I learn from hearing other people's perspectives on matters of importance to me. That's why I choose friends who will help me grow because they share the same values as me.

I used to avoid people with different interests than my own. But these days, I find different interests appealing. I've come to realize that if I only talk to people who share the exact same interests as me, all I "learn" is what I already know. By exposing myself to people with different interests, I hear things I never would have thought of. Are they all good ideas? Of course not—but out of three or four, if there is one gem, I benefit.

Some people may think I'm rude if I don't want to socialize with them, but honestly, it's my life, and I get to choose how I live it. I am not required to sacrifice my valuable time in order to make someone else feel good about themselves.

If you feel someone in your circle isn't on the same page as you or doesn't bring you sufficient value, it's okay to cut them loose. And do it without feeling guilty. For years, I wasted a lot of time allowing people to push and pull me in all different directions until I lost who I was.

Take the time to assess the people you spend the most time with. Ask yourself: "To what degree do they empower me to be the best I can be?" Then make the hard decision of what to do about the people who are a serious drain on your valuable productive time. Is it that person who keeps emailing you YouTube videos throughout the day, wanting you to watch them and comment *right now*? Is it the party-hard person who wants you to stay out all night with them, even though they won't head home until long after midnight, at which point they'll crash like a ton of bricks and sleep till noon?

Pruning my social circle wasn't easy. Feelings were hurt. But I knew there was nothing gained by sacrificing my feelings to take care of someone else's. So I let them go.

I know that sometimes you can't cut a time-drain person loose because they are a family member. What you can do, though, is reduce the amount of time you spend in their company. Then tell them the hard truth and let it be their responsibility to deal with it.

These days, my friendships support my lifestyle. For example, I can call my good friend David Meltzer at 4:30 AM to pitch him ideas. And I have several other friends who enjoy the early mornings like I do.

STEP TWO: Get a calendar or something you can use to track your days and record your progress. Many people I know use a computer program like Excel. I'm old-school—I use pen and paper and create multiple vision boards for my projects. I love to see everything in front of me. It reminds me of what I've accomplished and what remains to be done. I write lists constantly. I write down the time I train, when I eat, what and how much I read, and all my meetings and clients. I'm constantly jotting down notes and plans. This way, I don't get distracted.

Whichever method you choose, keeping track will keep you on point. It will show you where your valuable time is being spent. Are there too many distractions in your day? If so, cut them out—or at the very least, cut them down. However, if you see that you are mostly staying on track, good for you. Keep it up.

In an upcoming chapter, I will go into more tips for highly productive time management.

Revisit these five habits and be honest with yourself. Which habits do you already practice? And which habits do you need to start practicing?

Some people say they never have enough time, money, or resources. They think that if they had more of these things, only then would they be successful.

How about we flip that on its head?

A famous long-distance runner, Emil Zátopek is best known for winning three gold medals at the 1952 Summer Olympics in Helsinki, Finland. First, he won the five-thousand-meter and ten-thousand-meter runs. Then Zátopek decided to compete in the marathon at the last minute and won that, too. In his lifetime, he broke multiple world records while winning four Olympic gold medals and three European Athletics gold medals. Zátopek was nicknamed "The Czech Locomotive" for his relentless endurance.[14]

With little to no resources at his disposal, Zátopek's training techniques became legendary. The below-zero conditions of the Czechoslovakian winter would have stopped most runners from training, but not Zátopek. One day, during a blizzard when it was too cold to train outdoors, he made his own makeshift treadmill. He placed bath towels in his bathtub and ran a little warm water to soften them; then he stood in his bathtub and ran in one spot for over three hours. Zátopek said later that he envisioned himself streaking around the track as he was running in place in the tub.

To increase stamina, he also ran in army boots in the snow and rode his bike up hills with heavy weights on his back and legs. Zátopek believed that by training in this strenuous way, he could always outperform his competition when fiercely challenged during a long, grueling race.

Zátopek's training methods, although unorthodox at the time, have become famous. He also created his own style of what we now call HIIT (high-intensity interval training).

After Zátopek had achieved fortune as well as fame, a reporter found out how he trained and asked him, "Will you change your training regimen now that you can well afford to?"

Zátopek said no—he didn't need to depend on money or fancy equipment. He had enough self-discipline to continue relying on the bare minimum to achieve his goals.

Throughout the pandemic, many people have complained that they've had to spend too much time with themselves. Think about that. Some people don't want to spend time with their thoughts. Why is that?

There is always going to be an easy way out or a reason to quit. But what happens when we find a reason to keep going and stay the course? What happens when we buckle down and discipline ourselves to do the consistent, persistent work, day in and day out, no matter how we feel or the kinds of results we achieve? I'll tell you what happens: sooner or later, we succeed. We reach our goals. We end up turning a dream into a reality. No longer are we living in a fantasy of wishing or hoping for a lucky shot.

Yesterday's food doesn't keep us full today. If we only sweep the floor once, we'll eventually have a dirty floor again. The steady repetition of good thoughts and the right actions will *always* pay off. Is there an exception to this rule? Not if you resolutely maintain self-discipline.

HAVE A SPIRITUAL PLAN

Many people have a financial plan all worked out. They know what money is coming in and what's going out. Stocks and investments are all neatly figured out and regulated. Some people do it themselves; others with large portfolios usually hire someone. For some, financial planning is done monthly. Others, weekly. And for those with a lot at stake, daily.

But how many of you have a spiritual plan all worked out? I assure you, managing your spiritual plan (or spiritual life) is just as important as managing your financial accounts. In fact, I'd say that spiritual planning is integral to the final outcome of all your long-term financial plans. But more on this later.

"Spiritual" and "spirituality" are words people use all the time. Some people are put off by them, thinking they signal a holier-than-thou mentality. Others think that because they consider themselves to be spiritually minded, they are in a position to judge others. In other words, the gift of spirituality can just as easily be seen as a curse. From where I sit, the problem lies in people having a total misunderstanding of the concept—what it truly means to be spiritual. Because a truly spiritual person is absent of judgment toward other people. "Live and let live" is how they see it.

Spirituality does not have degrees. One person is not more spiritual than another. The good news is that spirituality is easy to attain. You don't have to work hard at it day in and day out. It's not like learning to play the piano. You don't have to practice, practice, practice, although the art of having a spiritual practice is where the reward lies. This is because spirituality is a mindset, a way of thinking—and, therefore, also a way of being. Your good actions match your good thoughts.

Some people confuse religion with spirituality. They believe you have to be religious to be spiritual. It's an ongoing misconception that causes so much conflict in the world today.

Since the beginning of time, we have been separating ourselves and fighting over what we believe to be right. But does it really matter? Does God or Spirit or Source, or whatever you want to call it, really care which path you take to end up in the same place? Is your God better than mine? Can my God beat up your God? Is that even a question worth asking? Do we really have to fight over all these theological ideas? Why can't we all just get along?

Spirituality is a very personal thing for unique individuals. It's not about unwavering devotion to a prescribed religious dogma. Spirituality is not about unquestioning loyalty to an omnipotent figurehead you piously believe in, either. Rather, it's about your devotion and loyalty to the rules and values (discussed earlier in this book) that you have created for yourself.

The last thing I want to do is tread on people's "belief toes," though. So let me preface everything you read here with "In my experience . . ."

Then you decide for yourself.

A spiritual person is someone who looks inside themselves for truth. They listen to their intuition no matter what is happening in the outside world. They are willing to do the work to discover who they are and what life means to them.

A spiritual person lives by high standards that are based on well-thought-out values and rules. They do not judge others for their opinions of reality because they know and understand that we all sort out information differently. A spiritual person does no harm to others or to the world around them. They honor the concept that we are all one. Thus, being kind to and taking care of others is no different from being kind to and taking care of yourself.

Sure, a spiritual person may have negative thoughts and may get angry. We are all human—but they take responsibility for their actions and make amends when they act inappropriately. A spiritual person understands there is a Source, Intelligence, or Energy that connects us all. And to be spiritual, we have to listen to that Source for daily guidance to be centered and adhere to our truth.

So ask yourself this: What do you believe being spiritual is, and why? Do you see yourself as a spiritual person? Do you think it's strange to talk about being spiritual?

Some people go to church on Sundays to pray. Some pray every day. Others pray "as needed." I think that kind of commitment is commendable, but does it make you a spiritual person? Really think about that. Is a priest or pastor more spiritual than you?

How about if that holy man or woman gives a pious sermon on Sunday and then acts inappropriately during the week when no one is watching? How about if someone goes to church every Sunday, and even goes to confession, yet they act badly or treat others unkindly on the other days of the week? Who really sets the standard of what is spiritual and what isn't? I think we can all agree that there needs to be a level of accountability in how you present yourself to the world.

A person who talks about good deeds while doing the exact opposite isn't being truly spiritual. I think words are cheap. We must become emotionally and socially intelligent and responsible to be truly spiritual and live life on a spiritual path.

I challenge you to answer these seven questions honestly:

- What do you want to achieve spiritually while here in on Earth?
- Why do you want to achieve this?
- How do you think you will feel once you achieve this?
- Do you believe you are a spirit having a human experience, or a human having a spiritual experience? Why?
- Do you feel you have a spiritual purpose in this life?
- If so, are you living it?
- If you aren't living it, what's stopping you?

Answering these questions honestly will help you take a look at your map of reality and find out, spiritually, how you can better get from where you are to where you want to be.

SEVEN HABITS THAT CAN HELP US BE MORE SPIRITUAL

1. BEING OF SERVICE

Before I got sober, being of service to others was never on my mind. My life was always about me, me, me—and what I could achieve or prove. Once sober, that all changed. I realized how important it is to give back to people. And this got me away from my scarcity mentality.

You don't have to overdo it. It's the thought that counts. But find a cause you believe in and support it to whatever degree you can. You could donate a little money or time to help an organization or someone in need. Perhaps you could mentor someone who needs some guidance or support. Assist an elderly neighbor; help a local high school sports team. There are so many ways to help others. It's very powerful, and the universe has always paid me back for the service work I have done. Not that I expect anything; it just does—and almost always in ways I never expected, such as someone doing a kindness for me that I didn't have to ask for.

2. FORGIVING PEOPLE WHEN THEY DO US HARM

It can be hard to forgive someone when they do us harm, but it's the only way we can be truly happy and healthy. We then get to live a life that isn't cluttered with grudges—and the need for paybacks. I wish I could say I'm a naturally forgiving person, but I'm not. I have to work on it every day, and trust me: some days are harder than others.

When we carry around old hurts, we aren't present in the moment. We become stuck in what happened yesterday, and we keep playing the old tapes that rule our lives. Once I realized that I can't change people—rather, I'm only responsible for the way I respond—I felt a massive relief. Now I see each day as a new day with new opportunities for me to learn and grow, free from the ball and chain of grudges.

3. BEING PATIENT

Having a newborn has tested my patience. I have to admit that my wife has way more patience than I do. I sometimes try to rush through things, but that never serves me well. Patience is an important discipline we must practice moment by moment. Patience is very powerful; in fact, it can be life changing. I remember when I first started writing and how impatient I was to get something finished. Then I would get back a round of edits and want to scream. Now I take a moment to sit down and enjoy the process of writing. It's important to STOP, breathe, and then take in and enjoy the moments in life. Having patience with my wife, son, friends, and clients is something that I have to continually work on; we all do. We can't create strong relationships and keep them if we don't have the patience to allow people to make mistakes and grow from them. And when we have patience, it encourages others to have patience with us.

4. BEING HONEST

Many people find it hard to be honest with themselves and with others. It is natural to have a fear of being rejected and to want the approval of others. But if we have to be dishonest to avoid rejection or get approval, is it really worth it in the end? What does it cost us in the long run if we live our lives dishonestly? I know that for me, the moment I lie to myself or others, I am going to get caught. Maybe not today. But lies are tenuous and have no substance—and they cannot hold up forever. I would rather be honest about my weaknesses than be afraid of them. For years, I lived in fear because I had reading and writing issues. I was embarrassed of them. But once I was open about my condition, people stepped up to help me. And that's the great thing about honesty: it attracts and keeps you in good company.

5. BEING GRATEFUL

We hear this all the time: "Be grateful for what you have—there is always someone out there with less than you." But the point of gratitude is to not look for lack anywhere. Not in yourself or in others. Rather, it's about being grateful for the blessings you already have, whether large or small, because this gratitude kicks in the law of attraction. I always start my day with noting three things I am grateful for. This helps me appreciate the little things that matter. Before I started doing this, I always felt that my life really wasn't going very well. Everything left a bad taste in my mouth. I was constantly complaining about everything and others. Today, I keep it very simple, and I'm grateful to have another day of living. Yep, living—because I know there are no guarantees.

6. FOLLOWING YOUR INTUITION

I'm all about following my gut. There is nothing wrong with needing information before you do something, but information alone is not always enough. For me, I go with my intuition, then fill in the details. Following my intuition is like being in a state of flow. I let go and just go. All great athletes and artists talk about the flow state. It was popularized by psychologist Mihaly Csikszentmihalyi in 1975.[15]. Being "in the flow" is described as a state where we are hyper-focused and not actually thinking. We are engaged in the moment so deeply that we let go of time and space and are just *being*. In a state of flow, you trust that the actions you are guided to do will naturally lead you to the best possible outcome. I have found that the more I trust my intuition, and the more I am in the flow, the happier I am with how things play out.

7. MEDITATING OR PRAYING TO CONNECT WITH INNER GUIDANCE

This has been part of my inner life for many years. There is no right or wrong way to pray or meditate. You can do it the classic way we so often think about: sitting quietly with one's eyes closed. But you can also meditate or pray while walking or running as long as you are being present. I suggest that you don't ask for things you want in a material way. Instead, ask for guidance and clarity. The universe is way more powerful than you can imagine. Trust and have faith. Clarity and insight will follow.

For me, the point of spirituality is that it will get you farther faster.

Lying, cheating, and stealing are quick fixes that may seem to put you on the fast track for success. However, these means to an end all have setbacks and serious consequences when you get caught. Some people make the mistake of thinking, *It's if I get caught*, as if they are magically protected or too smart to be found out. As if there is a sneaky way—and they are just clever enough to find it—to outwit fate.

There is a famous saying: "We are only as sick as our secrets." We all know when we are being honest with ourselves and with others. And in the end, that's what truly matters.

What so many people fail to realize is that the spiritual route is actually the easiest way to achieve any objective. Like the saying goes, if you are honest, you don't need to have a good memory. The truth is always the truth. It doesn't change. But if you lie, you have to remember each and every lie—or you'll get tripped up somewhere along the way.

But dishonest people look no farther than the lie—or the dishonesty. Their limited vision prevents them from seeing things any other way. They do not believe in consequences—until the ramifications of their dishonesty come home to roost. And even then, some people refuse to take responsibility for whatever mess they have perpetrated. A key to being spiritual is understanding the importance of taking responsibility for what we do and how our actions affect the lives of others, always making amends for our transgressions.

So why do so many people choose dishonesty? Because it has the illusion of being the easiest way. The way I see it, dishonest people are essentially lazy people. Since dishonesty appears to be that quick and easy solution for their problem or situation, they can use it to get what they want without having to do the honest work. But quick and easy is never going to make us truly happy in the long run. It solves a molehill today that will become a mountain tomorrow.

If they were to STOP or STAMP and play the dishonesty out to the final result, they would see that they have much more to lose by lying, cheating, or stealing. And they have so much more to gain by being forthright, gracious, and honest.

Spirituality at its essence is simply "Do the right thing." Ah, but what is the right thing? Let's say a situation presents itself to you. There's something you want, and there are two ways you can go about getting it. You can snatch it up by being dishonest. But then, will it truly be yours? Or will it only be yours up until you get caught?

Or, you can welcome it into your life, doing whatever it takes to achieve it, by being honest. In this case, it is absolutely yours to have and to hold onto.

Of course, some people will ask, "What if I want something badly, I do the honest work, and it still doesn't come to me?"

Well, in my experience, that only means one thing: there is something even better coming your way. And that something will be your reward for taking the spiritual approach.

As I've said before, we are all seeking pleasure and trying to avoid pain. But pain increases when we lie, cheat, or steal to attain pleasure. Conversely, pleasure is much more fulfilling in the long run when it is achieved through honest effort.

I wish I could tell you that shortcuts work, but they don't. I found out very early in my sobriety that the people who did the work every day were the ones who stayed sober, managed their lives, and were happy. I also discovered over the years that it's not how much time you spend doing something, it always comes down to the quality of the time you spend doing it.

The COVID-19 pandemic has tested me spiritually. Yes, at times I was tempted to take a few shortcuts, but I knew through past experiences that they would only leave me empty later on. You can live in a castle full of lies and look wealthy on the outside, but you'll be lost, alone, and full of fear on the inside.

Or you can be happy, have purpose, be of service, demonstrate honesty, and have integrity—and if so, you'll never feel overwhelmed. Money doesn't buy us spirituality, nor does fame. It takes the work we do on ourselves daily to grow in our thoughtfulness, to be the best person we can possibly be and thereby achieve the pure happiness that is our destiny.

Chapter 10

PARTING WORDS: CALL A TIME-OUT

When I was growing up, we seldom went on family vacations. My dad was a workaholic. He did his best with what he knew, which was putting a roof over our heads and food on the table. Unfortunately, it came at a price to his health and building a relationship with his kids. I competed in football and rugby and was a track star as a kid, but my dad put work first and never saw me run, not even once.

As a young adult, without really giving it any thought, I took on my dad's overwork ethic. I constantly pushed myself only to end up sick and run down. Then I got into drugs and alcohol, as you already know, to help me cope.

Once I caught on to my self-destructive conduct and subsequently got sober, only then did it occur to me that I had to make a change from my all-or-nothing work mode and enjoy some much-needed, replenishing time off.

Today, I make sure to spend time with my wife and son. I have spent more time with Orlando in three years than my father spent with me in eighteen years.

Work-wise, I have found that when I pace myself, the things I get done may not be as numerous as during my workaholic days, but they are of a much higher quality and are consequently more valuable or marketable. In sum, I still work hard, but I also make sure to play hard.

I have lived in NYC, Miami, LA, and Las Vegas. Traveled to Europe and got married in Paris. I have been to hundreds of live events and parties all over the world. I have competed in karate tournaments. I wanted to do stand-up comedy, so I had regular gigs at the Comedy Store in LA. I performed at the Laugh Factory, the Improv, Carolines on Broadway. I did it all. I feel like I've lived a hundred lives all in one.

But, as I said earlier, I didn't start out this way. I was consumed with both making money and making a name for myself. The restaurant nightlife business, though very lucrative, had me putting in sixteen-hour days and never coming up for air. I honestly never really liked the business, but the money was so good that I got stuck chasing the highs with little purpose or passion.

Over the years, I've had to break a lot of bad habits that were turning me into the same workaholic as my father. And if I'm not careful, not conscious, even today, sometimes I can get so involved in a project that I think of nothing else.

Fortunately for me, my wife and I are polar opposites. She absolutely loves to travel and enjoy life outside of work. She is a constant reminder of the importance of calling a time-out from work in order to have some fun. Thanks to Kim, I now look forward to trips abroad with the same enthusiasm as starting a new work project.

Having hobbies or fun interests and activities outside of work contributes to our spiritual, mental, and physical health. I know so many New Yorkers who never leave NYC or experience other cultures. I was trapped in that cycle for a long time.

It is essential that you get out and live a little. We all know how this movie called *Life* ends. Back in the day, when people would tell me about their recreational activities or the places they'd visited, I'd think to myself, *They're just wasting their time.* Now I look at the word "recreation" differently. It is the time we take to "re-create" ourselves. And this is valuable time spent. Many of my best ideas have occurred to me either during or right after this time-out. Consequently, the time I spend weight lifting, running, hiking, recording podcasts, and reading for pleasure isn't a waste; rather, it's an inspiration.

Today, step back and look at what you really want to experience. Open your mind to what's possible. Trust me, it's over before you know it. So let's think about those fun things you've wanted to do but keep putting off. I guarantee you won't regret it.

Here are a few things to open your mind to some fun and adventure . . .

Sports and Outdoor Adventures

Archery

Badminton

Basketball

Ballroom dancing

Bowling (lawn)

Bowling (tenpin)

Camping

CrossFit

Cycling

Fishing

Golf

Hiking

Horseback riding

Mountain biking

Paintball

Road trips

Rock climbing

Running (or walking)

Scuba diving

Skiing (snow or water)

Skydiving

Snowboarding

Surfing

Swimming

Table tennis

Tai chi

Tennis

Touch football

Volleyball

Whitewater rafting

Windsurfing

Yoga

Arts, Crafts, and Games

Acting

Bingo

Board games with family and/or friends

Book clubs

Cooking

Game nights with friends

Karaoke

Learning a craft	Poetry
Painting	Singing
Performing at open mics	Starting a blog or podcast
Photography	Video games (be careful not to
Playing an instrument	get hooked on this one)

Now I'm going to throw a challenge your way. In my line of work, I frequently find myself coaching workaholics and overachievers. I cannot tell you how many excuses I've heard when I tell them they need to start having more fun and suggest that they take up a sport or hobby for recreation. The most common excuse starts with: "It's too late in life for me to learn . . ." and ends with "a new sport" or "how to play an instrument," etc.

YOUR THIRTY-DAY CHALLENGE: THE AGGREGATION OF MARGINAL GAINS: THE 1 PERCENT RULE AND THE RIPPLE EFFECT

I recently read an excerpt from *Atomic Habits,* a book by James Clear, that really changed my perspective about achievement. Clear's premise is that small steps and the right focus create greatness.

At the start of the twenty-first century, the British Cycling organization decided to make a change by hiring a new performance director. Dave Brailsford was called upon to turn Britain's dreadful team and cycling culture around. At that time, Britain's cycling efforts were very average and had been for almost a century. Since 1908, Britain had only achieved one Olympic gold medal, and no British cycler had ever won the famous Tour de France, one of the toughest and most grueling cycling events in history.

Brailsford had an interesting approach; his philosophy focused on details, the 1 percent ripple effect, and small sequences adding up over time. He called it "the aggregation of marginal gains."[16]

Brailsford and his team started to make small changes. First, they redesigned the bike seats to make them more comfortable. He suggested riders wear heated shorts to keep their muscles warm. He experimented with different fabrics to see which one was the most aerodynamic.

From testing different massage gels to finding the most comfortable pillows and bedding to make sure his athletes got the right amount of rest, Brailsford was relentless with his strategy. But could all these small details really make a difference?

Five years after Brailsford started working with the team, the Brits won 60 percent of the medals at the 2008 Olympics. In 2012, in front of a home crowd, the Brits set nine Olympic records. Bradley Wiggins become the first Brit to win the Tour de France—and over the next six years, British athletes would win five more times.

Most people never pay attention to the small details and how important they are. But let's take Clear's example of a plane heading from Los Angeles to New York City in a straight line. A slight one-degree turn in either direction at the start will take us dramatically off course over a five-hour trip. How about the ripple or compound effect of a bad spending habit, overeating, excessive drinking, or taking drugs? How far off course do you think it will take you over time?

When I was running with Orlando, training for the half-marathons, I'd see a gentleman out walking every morning. I began calculating how far I was running and how far he was walking. My guess was he was doing at least seven miles a day. Finally, I was so curious that one day I stopped him and asked.

He said, "I walk eight miles a day."

He looked to be around fifty-five, and I asked him, "How old are you?"

He replied, "I'm seventy-two."

Now, here is the kicker: I said, "You must have been pretty fit as a kid, and it's so great you've kept it up."

He shook his head. "Not at all. I started walking at sixty-five. After I retired and was eighty pounds overweight, my doctor said that at this rate, I had two years to live."

He wasn't a big guy—about 5'6" and maybe 160 pounds, so adding eighty pounds to his small frame would have indeed been a stressor on his heart.

He went on to say, "I was so unfit, I could barely tie my shoes or make it up a flight of stairs. It took me sixty days to be able to walk one mile."

Imagine that: now he's seventy-two and walking over fifty miles a week.

Small, focused attention in the right direction will always make a massive difference. Think about how far you would travel if you started to walk every day for an hour. Or, at an hour a day, how many books you could read. Or, practicing an hour a day, what new, fun thing (a sport, an instrument, etc.) you could learn.

So here is your thirty-day challenge: just take one thing that would give you joy and commit to working or playing at it for one hour a day over the next thirty days.

What is that thing that gets you excited, that you would be happy and proud to master—or even be fair to middling at—but, by making excuses, you've put off for far too long?

Stop merely talking about it. Stop overthinking it. Whatever it is, like Nike says, just do it!

This book you are holding in your hands emerged out of one sentence that came to me in 2017. I heard someone say, "The difference between ordinary and extraordinary people is that the extraordinary person is prepared to do a little extra than the average or ordinary person." When I reflected on this, I realized I frequently looked for shortcuts or the easy way out to get things done. I knew it was time to show people how to get a positive DOSE in life, no matter what we are faced with.

When I first put pen to paper, there were a lot of emotions and uncertainty running through me along the lines of, "Can I really do this?" But once I started writing, even though I didn't know each day what to expect, I fell in love with the process. Then something just clicked, and I let go. It was as if I didn't know I was writing a book. I just knew I needed to empower others and help them find their potential. And this is how it played out:

A sentence turned into a paragraph. The paragraphs became a page. The pages accumulated into a chapter. And the chapters compiled into a book.

As I said, it wasn't what I expected when the idea first came to me. But I simply set aside an hour a day to write, and over time, it all came together.

I can look at my past and pinpoint where I didn't do the small work that I needed to do to accomplish something that was important to me. But I don't do that anymore. If it is something that gives me joy, and I will be less than I am capable of for not doing it, I put in the small increments to make it happen.

I now commit to the process and have faith that if I do the work, I will reap what I sow. It's not always easy, but once I get started, I build momentum.

As you're reading this, I'm telling you that anyone who says you can't reach your full potential is a liar and a fool. I'm not special or gifted, so if I can do it, so can you. Don't worry about money or resources. Use what you have in front of you and start. That's it; just start. The work you *don't* do, without question, *never* gets done. The work you *start*, though, has a chance of becoming something great. You don't need magic pills or miracles. Just get going. Find your joy that complements your work. Not next week. Not tomorrow. Right after you read this sentence.

EPILOGUE

"We are visitors on this planet. We are here for one hundred years at the very most. During that period we must try to do something good, something useful, with our lives. If you contribute to other people's happiness, you will find the true meaning of life."

Tenzin Gyatso, the fourteenth Dalai Lama

Wait a minute . . . what's this? Only *novels* have an epilogue! You know, the part that tells you how the main character's life turned out—usually some time after the main events of the story have passed.

Well, right now, I want you to think about *your* epilogue. Where are you going to be—*who* are you going to be—a year from now? And why?

Unfortunately, many people finish reading a self-help book and put it down, unaffected—and then go about living their same old life. They expect to be changed for simply having read the words on the pages. As if the text, in and of itself, will magically transform them without them having to take any action. And if they're not changed, they think, *Oh well; maybe the next book I read will do the trick!*

I took you on quite a journey in this book. If you have made it this far, congratulations! Take a breath and give yourself a pat on the back. You have done what a lot of people won't, don't, or can't do. Anyone can start a book, just like anyone can join a gym as a New Year's resolution. But only a small percentage do the actual work, day in and day out, to reach the end and achieve the benefits. But here's the thing: you—yes, *you*—are different. I know that for a fact because here you are, still in the game.

I got brutally honest with you about my past so you could see, uncut and uncensored, where I have come from and what is possible. I believe in you. You got this far without quitting. And if you are willing to believe in yourself and *do the work*, then you're capable of living an extraordinary and empowered life. If you have any doubts, *stop*. Remember, I'm not special. I don't have any rare talent. I struggle with my dyslexia every day. I also have to work on my recovery daily. Furthermore, I have chronic ADHD and was told by more people than I care to remember: "You'll never amount to anything in life, Michael Diamond!" Like my good friend David Meltzer once said, "People assumed you were stuck in stupid."

But guess what? They couldn't see what I have and what each of you have: a cache of potential. I know you're amazing and that you can unleash your full potential right now. Yes, right now.

Use the techniques I have provided. Get flexible in your mindset and discard any remnants of your fixed mindset. Maintain a positive outlook on life. Know your purpose—your "why." Create values and rules that empower you. Find the right place instead of waiting for it to find you. Surround yourself with Engines—people who put wind in your sails and keep you on your toes—and dump the Anchors in your life. And remember that the best master plans tap into the bigger energy of the universe.

Be obsessed—yes, obsessed—with the future you want to create. And let go of the past: it's dead to you, starting today. This is your call to action. Whatever it is that inspires you, start doing and reaching for it now, as soon as you put this book down. Start small. Remember the power of the 1 percent and how it compounds, moment by moment. Learn a new language. Start a course online. Learn to play an instrument. Find your joy and exploit it. You have nothing to lose, and you have the rest of your life to enjoy the rewards of your effort.

Like I have said over and over (and will continue to say again and again): successful people do the work no matter how they feel. Unsuccessful people only work when they feel good. Live big, live grand, and release the power and potential in you.

It's time to take your DOSE of positivity and shine!

ACKNOWLEDGMENTS

Sometimes a thank-you is so large that it has to come in the form of a story.

On March 11, 2020, I was blessed to meet David Meltzer when he interviewed me on his podcast, *The Playbook*. David and I hit it off the moment we met. After the podcast, I asked David if he wanted to collaborate with me by doing a weekly live show together, and David jumped at the idea. The show has now been running for three years and has become a syndicated show that airs on Bloomberg and Apple TV.

Little did I know that a week after meeting David, the world we once knew would change forever as we were put in lockdown due to the global spread of COVID-19.

Once we went into lockdown, I put pen to paper. A lot of emotions were running through me. I didn't know that what I was writing at the time would become the book you are reading now.

As the pages piled up, I reached out to my first cousin, Despene Sattler, who I knew I could trust, as she has known me all my life. I sent her the first ten thousand words that had, it felt, fallen out of me. Despene encouraged me to keep writing and offered to be my first editor.

We got busy. Within eight weeks, draft one of *A Dose of Positivity* was completed. I wasn't sure what to do next, so I called David Meltzer, who put me in touch with his editor, Cliff Carle. Cliff loved the first draft, and together we went to work on the second.

After a grueling six-month rewrite, I went searching for an agent and had no luck for twelve months. After multiple rejections from agents and publishers, I was frustrated. I didn't know what direction to take the manuscript to best bring it out in the world. I decided to take a chance and emailed super-agent Bill Gladstone. Bill changed the course of my life. After reading the manuscript, he decided to represent me even though he wasn't taking on any new authors. I will be forever grateful to Bill for taking a chance on me.

With Bill's connections, I landed a publishing deal with the incredible Matt Holt, who has his imprint through the amazing team at BenBella Books, which works with the distribution team at Penguin Random House. I can't express the level of gratitude I have for everyone at Matt Holt Books and BenBella for turning my dream into a reality. To my editing, marketing, and production team—Gregory Newton Brown, Katie Dickman, Lydia Choi, Mallory Hyde, Kerri Stebbins, Kim Broderick, Brigid Pearson, and everyone else—I can't thank you all enough.

Over the years, many people have helped me on this journey, whether they are aware of it or not. Some people I have known for many years, and others for only a few. But all of them have become part of my extended spiritual family. This list isn't in any particular order, but all these people have helped me reach my full potential, been unconditional in accepting me when it mattered most, and shaped me into the person I am today. Thank you to Des and Jerry Incollingo, John Grimanes, Judy Turner, Maria Hucker, Len Fode, Renae Denness, Michael Ault, Matthew Arden, David Sarner, Tony Theodore, Ana Roman, Jona Genova, Danny Nucci, Robert Montwaid, Paul Hughes, Dara Samuelson, Peter Macmilan, Theresa Macmilan, Jason Strauss, Justin Levine, Francis Milon, Eric Milon, Vanessa Adamou, Michael Mortan, Marc Live Giveand, Rob Hannley, John Stamos, Scott Weiland, Brett Scallion, Duff Mckagan, Andy Belmonti, Robert Steinberg, John Eaton, Aaron Knowles, Jennifer Buonantony, Charlie Smith, Morgan Spurlock, Donavan Warren, Cliff Carle, and Despene Sattler.

Finally, I would like to thank my parents, Nick and Julie Diamond, for teaching me to be resilient, gritty, and driven. I also want to thank my father- and mother-in-law, Tennyson Jay Kwok and Erlinda Ortiz Kwok, for always helping out and being there. And, of course, thank you to my wife, Kimberly, who allows me to be myself and never tells me my dreams are crazy. Kim, you support me when I need it the most, and you are amazing. Finally, thank you, Orlando, for choosing me as your father. Your dynamic, energetic, and magical spirit is incredible. You have given me purpose and life and taught me to be a better person and do better in the world every day.

ENDNOTES

1   Linda Stryker, "Meditation and the Mind," *Emeritus Voices*, Emeritus College at Arizona State University, accessed July 8, 2022, https://emerituscollege.asu.edu/sites/default/files/ecdw/EVoice10/meditation_and_mind.html.

2   "Donald Hebb," The Decision Lab, accessed July 8, 2022, https://thedecisionlab.com/thinkers/neuroscience/donald-hebb.

3   D.O. Hebb, *The Organization of Behavior: A Neuropsychological Theory* (New York: Routledge, Taylor & Francis Group, 2012).

4   Brian Wansink and Jeffery Sobal, "Mindless Eating: The 200 Daily Food Decisions We Overlook," *Environment and Behavior* 39, no. 1 (January 2007): 106–23, doi:10.1177/0013916506295573.

5   "10 Best Ways to Increase Dopamine Levels Naturally," Healthline, accessed July 8, 2022, https://www.healthline.com/nutrition/how-to-increase-dopamine.

6   "12 Dopamine Supplements to Boost Your Mood," Healthline, accessed July 8, 2022, https://www.healthline.com/nutrition/dopamine-supplements.

7   "Exercise Is Good for Your Brain's Gray Matter," *Neuroscience News*, January 2, 2020, https://neurosciencenews.com/exercise-gray-matter-15374/.

8   Mary Bellis, "Famous Thomas Edison Quotes," ThoughtCo, July 3, 2019, https://www.thoughtco.com/edison-quotes-1991614.

9   Viktor E. Frankl, *Man's Search for Meaning* (Boston: Beacon Press, 2006).

10 Rae Jacobson, "4 Reasons I Think Albert Einstein May Have Had Dyslexia," Understood, July 16, 2017, https://www.understood.org/en /articles/albert-einstein-dyslexia.

11 *Bethany Hamilton: Unstoppable*, directed by Aaron Lieber (2018; distributed by Netflix).

12 Kevin Kruse, "The 80/20 Rule and How It Can Change Your Life," *Forbes*, March 7, 2016, https://www.forbes.com/sites/kevinkruse/2016 /03/07/80-20-rule/?sh=3b5a17113814.

13 Angel E. Navidad, "Marshmallow Test Experiment and Delayed Gratification," Simply Psychology, November 27, 2020, https://www .simplypsychology.org/marshmallow-test.html.

14 "Emil Zatopek," Olympics.com, accessed July 8, 2022, https://olympics .com/en/athletes/emil-zatopek.

15 Mihaly Csikszentmihalyi, *Flow: The Psychology of Optimal Experience* (New York: HarperCollins, 2008).

16 James Clear, "This Coach Improved Every Tiny Thing by 1 Percent and Here's What Happened," JamesClear.com, accessed July 8, 2022, https://jamesclear.com/marginal-gains.

ABOUT THE AUTHOR

Mike Diamond is an author, television personality, and interventionist. Over the last decade Mike has become one of the top addiction interventionists in the country and has helped hundreds of people get sober. He is a certified NLP practitioner and has toured the nation as a keynote speaker, spreading his empowering message of hope and positivity.

GET YOUR DOSE OF POSITIVITY

For more daily, weekly, and monthly Doses of Positivity to keep you inspired, educated, and motivated to live your potential and best life.

You can listen to podcasts and watch inspirational videos from Mike by visiting

https://themikediamond.com/.